MIKE —
BELIEVE IN PEOPLE MORE
THAN THEY BELIEVE IN
THEMSELVES!

"THE OLD GUY"

LITTLE
LEADERSHIP
LESSONS

•••

FROM AN OLD GUY

by GLENN VAN EKEREN

Imprint: Independently published

For information regarding permission or distribution, contact
gvanekeren@vhs.com

To discover more about the author visit **enthusedaboutlife.com**

ISBN: 978-1-7350962-0-9

A Word Of Thanks From The Old Guy

I'm so grateful for the countless people who have been an encouragement in my professional career.

Thank you to mentors who lovingly guided my path yet gave me the freedom to think, learn and grow on my own.

Thank you to professional colleagues whose passion for excellence challenged me to never settle for good enough.

Thank you to leaders who believed in me, encouraged me to stretch my expectations and gave me the confidence to pursue my potential.

A special thank you to the team members I've been privileged to lead. You taught me the value of serving, caring and doing what's right for people.

One's career is rarely fulfilling without a family's unconditional acceptance and sometimes silent motivation that communicates; "You can do it!" Thank you family!

A note from the old guy...

"I Love People!"

"Why are they so needy?"

"It's exciting to encourage self-motivated people."

"How can they be so high maintenance?"

"It's so fun to watch her chase her potential."

"What was he thinking?"

"That was a great conversation."

"I can't read their mind!"

Such is the internal conversation and mixed emotions of anyone leading people. One day, it is the most exciting job and privilege in the world. The next day, you're wondering why you aspired to be a leader.

Welcome to the world of leading people. It's messy!

I recommended to our Chief People Officer that we write a book filled with the people issues she deals with every day. We considered entitling it: The Complicated, Crazy and Comical World of People. We ultimately concluded the reader would think we were writing a fictional novel. Certainly, these stories of people issues couldn't be true.

But they are!

Humans are complex, complicated and at times a comical mix of attitudes, emotions and behaviors.

Admittedly, sometimes there is seemingly no rhyme or reason for people's success or failure for that matter. And, with some, their future success or failure is as clear as a painting on the wall.

It's crazy!

People are Magical and Mystical!

Your impact can be Monumental!

Leaders need to believe they can make a significant impact and difference in people's lives. This investment is tricky. Sometimes the returns are not what we expect. Some people blossom at breakneck speed while others are slow to mature. Some investments even go south for awhile but like the stock market, they normally recover.

Remember, people want to do good things. Most people don't get up in the morning wondering how they can make someone else's day difficult. They don't look in the mirror on their way to work and ask: "How can I mess things up today?"

Problem People are the minority, not the majority. Never allow the actions, attitudes or performance of one person determine how you treat everyone. In other words, just because one person might disappoint you don't let their behavior impact how you treat everyone else.

People inherently want to be appreciated and liked, loved, and valued. Treat people like they make a difference and they will. As leaders, we show people their worth and how it can be invested.

In my early days as a leader, I was advised not to get 'too close' to those I supervised. Keep your distance. You can't be friends with those you lead.

Maybe.

Here's what I know after 45 years of leadership. You must like people. You must know people. You must believe in people. You must see the best in people. You must hold people's hands. You must inspire people. You must be there for people and you must have a relationship with people...

You've got to love people more than polices, paper or profit.

People with passion can make the impossible possible. Leaders can't produce the passion, but you can do what it takes for people to feel passionate about what they do and the contribution they make.

That's what this book is all about. . . enjoy the people journey.

Believe In People

...More Than they Believe In Themselves.

One of the most powerful ways for leaders to impact the lives of people is to believe in people more than they believe in themselves. The first step in believing in people is to see them as a precious treasure waiting to be fully discovered. As Ken Blanchard so aptly said:

"Everyone you meet is a potential winner; some are disguised as losers. Don't be fooled by their appearances."

I was a young, naïve, wet behind the ears, energetic twenty-eight-year-old ready to take on the challenges of being the Director of Personnel for an organization of 125 people. To complicate matters, I had very little self-confidence and found myself struggling daily with feelings of inadequacy. Fortunately, my energy and enthusiasm made up for most of my lack of experience and ignorance.

Unfortunately, these feelings weren't new. I'd been living with them since I was a young troublemaker in elementary school. (I decided negative attention was better than no attention at all and my grades certainly weren't gaining me much positive attention). Here I was in a position of responsibility and it seemed everyone around me had wonderful talent, exceptional insights and seemingly incredible knowledge that I lacked. Poor me!

Bob was my Executive Director, mentor and friend. Driving to an out of town meeting one day I was lamenting all my shortcomings, weaknesses, and inferiority while bemoaning the fact I didn't have what others had. Then, it happened. Bob said something I'd never heard before. "Glenn, I believe in you. That's why I hired you. When are you going to start using the abilities you have and quit comparing yourself to other people? You have talents they don't have. It's time for you to make a difference. I expect impressive results."

No one had ever communicated their belief in me quite that way. It was personal, direct and sincere. Bob backed it up with support, direction, correction, encouragement and a periodic kick in the pants. He complimented me in public. He corrected me in private. He let me know he expected great things from me and gave me the freedom to implement new ideas, make tough decisions and nurture a culture that was right for people.

My experience must be exactly what Sam Walton was referring to when he said:

"Outstanding leaders go out of the way to boost the self-esteem of their personnel. If people believe in themselves, it's amazing what they can accomplish."

"Glenn, I believe in you" transformed my life. I'm convinced we can help people achieve new levels of performance by believing in them more than they believe in themselves. I've experienced it! I've lived it! And, I'm convinced believing in people is a critical tool in the leader's tool chest.

I fully endorse the great historian and poet Ralph Waldo Emerson's belief that if we

"Treat people greatly they will show themselves great."

Questions to Ponder:

1. How can you go about expressing your belief in people?

2. How can you treat people 'great?'

3. Who is waiting to hear you say, "I believe in you?"

Get It Right

Creating Culture Is A Concentrated, Conscious Choice.

I believe with all my heart as Tony Hsieh (Zappos CEO) does that, "If you get the culture right, most of the other stuff will just take care of itself."

If I put 500 leaders in a room and asked how many believed that a good work environment was important to their business' success, I suspect a majority would agree.

There is a significant difference between recognizing the importance of a good culture and knowing how to create it or being willing to invest the time and energy to make it happen.

I've discovered that creating a positive, high-performing, people-focused, result producing environment doesn't come naturally. It takes an incredible leadership investment. Unfortunately, leaders often find a vibrant company culture an elusive quest.

Where do we begin?

Good to Great author Jim Collins once said,

"Change doesn't begin with a vision. It begins with facing the brutal facts."

I don't know about you, but I find that conclusion convicting. Here's what we can do:

Begin with a frank assessment of your current culture. Is it chaotic or focused, formal or relaxed? Is the culture vibrant or boring? Would you say people are energized or drained? Stimulating or stuffy? Friendly or uninviting? The culture descriptive adjectives go on infinitum.

Then what? Keep in mind...

You Have a Culture. Like it or not. Intentional or unintentional. Desirable or undesirable. Every company has a culture. Leaders decide the level of influence they will inject into their culture. A leader's attention to culture is the difference maker between a vibrant and a struggling, stymied environment.

Make Culture a Priority. So many times, I've encountered leaders who believe giving attention to building the culture is important... so long as we have the time.

The tyranny of the urgent often takes priority over people.

There is a "Once... Then" mentality. Once we get everything else taken care of, people will be our priority.

Pay Attention. Culture is movable, fluctuating, shifting. It requires continual attention, nurturing, direction and adjustments. Culture doesn't function well on automatic pilot. It flourishes when leadership is continually passionate about infusing culture with their influence.

Be There for People. I'm reminded of an exchange between Pooh and his dear friend Piglet in A.A. Milne's Winnie the Pooh:

Piglet sidled up to Pooh from behind. "Pooh?" He whispered. "Yes, Piglet?" "Nothing," said Piglet, taking Pooh's hand. "I just wanted to be sure of you."

Simply knowing you are there. You have their back and support their best interest. Your presence brings calm and confidence during crisis. You nurture their creativity and passion to contribute. These are the things culture is made of. Be there for people.

A Word of Caution: Leaders, it is impossible for us to create, nurture, grow and sustain a dynamic work environment if paper trumps the people priority.

You can't build people if you remove yourself from them. You can't build culture if you are disconnected from it.

A dynamic culture doesn't happen accidentally. If you want a great place to work, it will take a conscious, concentrated effort to make it a reality.

_____

Questions to Ponder:

1. How would I describe our current culture? More importantly, how would our team describe the current culture?
2. What is the current priority – people or paper? How can you measure it?
3. What one thing can I do to make a positive impact on our work environment?

Maintain High Standards

**If Your Team Was Just Like You,
Would You Be Proud Of Their Efforts?**

Lou Holtz expected a lot from his football players. He also demanded
a lot from himself as their leader. "I won't accept anything less than
the best a player's capable of doing. . ." he said. "And he has the right to
expect the best that I can do for him and the team!"

Here are a few high standards I encourage every leader to employ,
expect and exhibit.

Outlaw apathy.

It's not just what we do but the spirit with which we do things that
matters. Leaders who grudgingly walk through the day – although
compliant and competent – will struggle to endear the respect of their
team. Be willing to activate a positive, passionate leadership example or
be ready for less than spectacular results from your followers.

I have a very low tolerance for apathy. Team members should be able to depend on us to portray a continual picture of what the environment should look like, feel like and be like. It's not just "what" we do. The "manner" in which we do it has the greatest impact. Grudging compliance and a vibrant "Yes, I Can" attitude are miles apart. Leave no doubt which path you're traveling.

Be willing to say: "I was wrong, I'm sorry."

In his book with Ken Blanchard, Everyone's a Coach, Don Schula tells of losing his temper near an open microphone during a televised game with the Los Angeles Rams. Millions of viewers were surprised and shocked by Shulas's explicit profanity. Letters soon arrived from all over the country, voicing the disappointment of many who had respected the coach for his integrity.

Shula could have played the "excusiology" card, but he didn't. No excuses. Everyone who included a return address received a personal apology. He finished each letter by saying, "I value your respect and will do my best to earn it again."

Leaders make mistakes. They fail. No big deal. Set the example. Make no excuses. Own the mess. Apologize to the team. Learn from the failure, correct it, and move on.

Ignite the Fire.

There's an old Texas saying, "You can't light a fire with a wet match." How's your enthusiasm, passion quotient? Is there a fire in your belly? Danny Cox believes, "The important thing to remember is that if you don't have that inspired enthusiasm that is contagious, whatever you do have is also contagious."

Passion driven leaders make things happen by inspiring others with their energy and commitment - passion. They create a culture where people love coming to work, look forward to the next opportunity and are willing to invest their mind and heart in making the organization a great place to be. This is a highly contagious spirit every leader should strive to nurture in herself and others. The leader's enthusiasm will inevitably spill over and magnetize followers.

Jim Collins author of Good to Great said:

"You can't manufacture passion or 'motivate' people to feel passionate. You can only discover what ignites your passion and the passions of those around you."

Be the spark plug. Ignite the fire in you and others will follow. At least get the pilot light going.

The leader must be willing to radiate positive energy and expectations whether things are going great or times are tough. It just goes with the territory.

Set high expectations.

I will do whatever it takes to help someone be successful except one thing – lower the standards. "We expect our leaders to be better than we are," declared Paul Harvey, "or why are we following them." We expect a lot from team members and they have every right to expect a lot from leadership.

In her autobiography, And So It Goes, Linda Ellerbee, then anchor of NBC News Overnight, wrote about a letter she once received from a little girl. It said: "Dear Miss Ellerbee, When I grow up I want to do exactly what you do. Please do it better."

Dear Leader. If your team was just like you, would you be proud of their efforts?

Fight complacency like a plague.

If you worked for you would you be inspired by your standards? I find the higher the expectations I have for myself the easier it is to encourage others to raise the bar for their results. "Make your personal standard of performance – your behavior in all areas," stated John Wooden, "so exemplary that those under your supervision will find it hard to match, harder to surpass."

When you stand strong for a continual higher standard, without waffling or wavering, the message will soon be clear.

Highly effective leaders promote and display unusually high standards.

_____

Questions to Ponder:

1. What standards would my team say are important to me?
2. How have I modeled those behaviors for my team?

Finding the Sweet Spot

**Don't Try To Change What People Are.
Develop What They Have.**

———————————

Strengths expert Marcus Buckingham asserted, "The corporate world is appallingly bad at capitalizing on the strengths of its people."

Leaders could undoubtedly learn from what legendary basketball Coach John Wooden did to help his players improve their shooting percentages. "I observed [as they practiced], I watched them," he said. "And when I found their spot, I went out there and drew a circle and said, 'This is where you shoot from; this is where you make your shot.'"

What a simple strategy!

Find out what people are good at and find a way to let them do more of it.

Wooden simply watched. What he observed enabled him to help his players achieve their full potential. He helped them perform in their 'sweet spot' at their highest level.

The perpetual privilege of every leader is to identify and nurture the God-given talents of their team members. NBA coach Pat Riley learned: "Every member of a team plays a different role and brings different skills." The leader's job is to find it and develop it.

I love the story about the little girl coming home after her first day in first grade and told her dad, "my teacher told me I was like the center of an apple. Here, cut this apple in half and let's see."

As the father started to cut the apple vertically, the little girl interrupted; "no daddy, you have to cut it the right way (horizontally) to see the real me." Once cut the "right way" there was a star in the center.

The "right way" to reveal the star in people is to

develop what God has left in someone instead of trying to put in what God has left out.

Human nature loves to identify the missing pieces in people's lives but seems mystified by the tremendous power and possibilities of building on what God has already provided.

The most productive thing we can do for our team members is to help people understand their talents, gifts and natural abilities. In other words,

Don't try to change what people are, develop what they have.

I remind myself every day to develop what God has left in someone instead of trying to put in what God left out. Human nature loves to identify the missing pieces in people's lives but seems mystified by the tremendous power and possibilities of building on what God provided. What if? What if a leader invested their energies in making people's weaknesses (missing pieces) irrelevant by making their strengths stronger? I'm an avid proponent of Marcus Buckingham's belief that, "The best strategy for building a competitive organization is to help individuals become more of who they are."

Don't try to change what people are but develop what they have.

_____

Questions to Ponder:

1. Do I know the 'sweet spot' of my team members?
2. Have told them what I think their 'sweet spot' is?
3. How can I set them up to do more of what they do well?

Simplifying Communication

Know. Feel. Do.

Kellen Wilkes offered this simple definition of communication: "Communication is the effective transfer of information between individuals that results in a commonly shared understanding of the issues at hand."

Simple enough. Easier said than done.

Alan Greenspan, Federal Reserve Chairman, before speaking on the economy to the 323rd meeting of the Economic Club of New York said, "I guess I should warn you, if I turn out to be particularly clear, you've probably misunderstood what I've said."

Effective communication is complicated. In its simplest form, there are three answers I need to answer:

What Do I Want People to Know?

Leaders must be crystal clear on the information they deliver and never leave information, directions or expectations up for interpretation.

My wife and I recently returned from vacation on a late-night flight. Our son-in-law agreed to bring our car to the airport and leave it in the parking ramp.

Josh sent me a text with pictures and explicit directions to the car. His directions simply read: take the walkway that's the farthest down (north most) into the parking garage. On the 3rd level in the garage, take a right and walk towards the spiral exit (to the north). Your car is then just a few spots west of the spiral exit.

Unfortunately, his intent and my interpretation were not the same and I wandered aimlessly in the parking garage looking for our vehicle. Side note: it was 5 degrees above zero with 30 mile an hour wind. **Cold!**

I learned that delivering clear, succinct directions is sometimes much easier than interpreting them. Always remember this valuable insight: A message sent is only as good as the receiver's perception of it.

Secondly,

What Do I Want People To Feel?

We often forget to appeal to people's emotions. To speak to their heart. Do I want people to feel challenged, encouraged, inspired or just informed? What is the best way to touch those emotions?

Finally,

What Do I Want People To Do?

Just because you said it, doesn't mean they heard it, comprehended it, believe it or plan to do anything with it.

Several years ago, a seasoned plumber wrote to the U.S. Bureau of Standards promoting a few acceptable procedures for cleaning pipes. The bureau replied: "The efficiency of the recommended solution is completely undisputed. However, there is an inherent incompatibility between the aforementioned solution and the basic chemical structures of the commonly used materials in current household and commercial pipeworks."

The plumber immediately wrote back saying, "thanks, I really liked it, too."

Within a few days, the Bureau responded with another letter: "Don't use hydrochloride acid! It eats holes in pipes!"

Know. Feel. Do. Be Clear!

_____

Questions to Ponder:

Set up an agenda for your next team meeting. Ask:

1.   What Do I Want People To Know?
2.   What Do I Want People To Feel?
3.   What Do I Want People To Do?

Organize the conversation around this information.

Don't Zap People

Infuse People's Self Esteem With Confidence

As a young boy, I enjoyed spending summer hours on my grandparents' farm. Not only did I have a great time with my grandparents, I learned a lot about life . . . and leadership (even though I certainly didn't know it at the time).

On a walk to the pasture one morning to bring in the milk cows for milking, grandpa and I came face to face with an electric fence. (For you non-farming readers, electric fences are a single strand of wire strung around a piece of land usually containing livestock. And, it provides a powerful electric shock when a body encounters it.)

Face-to-face with the wire, my grandpa looked around, then placed a hand on the wire to steady himself, and stepped over it. It was a mysterious event for a young boy who had suffered the 'shocking' effects of being zapped.

As we returned from the pasture I was overcome with curiosity. "Why did you look around before stepping over the wire?" I asked Grandpa. "And for that matter, why have an electric fence if you're not going to turn on the power?"

Grandpa smiled and said, "I was just looking to see if any cattle were watching me as I approached the fence. Never give them an idea of what they might be able to do. Electric fences don't need to be left on all the time. Once cattle learn they will be zapped, they will graze right up to the fence and stop." Then he pointed to the different heights of grass on the two sides of the tiny wire.

I've been zapped. How about you? Ever had a crazy idea you wanted to try and were told you needed to be realistic? Ever dream about improving a process only to have someone remind you dreaming is not your job? Have you ever been desperate for your supervisor's support to try something new only to be told to follow the rules? If so, you've been zapped.

Have you ever done any of the above to anyone else? You've been the zapper!

Groupon founder, Andrew Mason advised: "Hire great people and give them the freedom to be awesome." Giving people the freedom, encouragement and boost to be awesome is impossible if I'm a Zapper. I have found one of the simplest leadership actions we can activate to help team members pursue Awesome is:

Find a Way to Say Yes!

Tell people to give it their best shot. Go for it! Encourage dreaming and melting the status quo. Use encouragement to infuse people's self-esteem with confidence.

Questions to Ponder:

1. How do people on your team get zapped? Have you zapped anyone lately?

2. How can you encourage the creativity, innovation, risk-taking spirit of your team members?

Tickets of Recognition

If You See Something Good, Say Something Good.

According to the Chicago Tribune, in 1993 the police in South Windsor, Connecticut, pulled over a larger number of motorists than ever.

What's up with that?

One person stopped by a patrolman was Lori Carlson. As the officer approached her car, she was puzzled at what she had done wrong. To her amazement (and relief), the officer handed her a ticket that read, "Your driving was GREAT! – and we appreciate it."

In early June, authorities in the Hartford suburb began a program to give safe drivers a two-dollar reward for obeying the speed limit, wearing seat belts, having children in safety seats and using their turn signals.

"You are always nervous when you see the police lights come on," said

Carl Lomax, another South Windsor resident pulled over for good driving. It takes a second or two to adjust to the officer saying, 'Hey, thanks a lot for obeying the law.' It's about the last thing you would expect."

The officers of South Windsor had a novel idea – thank people for doing right.

A novel idea indeed! Any chance we could transfer that mindset into the workplace?

"Recognition is so easy to do and so inexpensive to distribute," advised Rosabeth Moss Kanter, "that there is simply no excuse for not doing it."

That is simply so undeniably true!

Is recognition of a job well done one of the last things our team members would expect from us? I'm feeling a bit convicted. . .

A 1989 article in Fortune magazine talked about the business secrets of Los Angeles Dodgers manager Tommy Lasorda. He said, "I want my players to know that I appreciate what they do for me [and] that I depend on them. When you, as a leader of people, are naïve enough to think that you, not your players, won the game, then you're in bad shape."

Recognition becomes (more) natural when a leader sincerely recognizes that the team, not them, is responsible for their success. It's their dedication, unselfish effort and Yes, I Can attitude that makes the leader look good.

Jim Collins, of Good to Great fame, said:

"Look in the window, not the mirror, to apportion credit for the success of the company."

Questions to Ponder:

1. When is the last time you issued a 'ticket of recognition?'
2. Who needs to hear that what they are doing is making a difference?

Who's Your One in a Hundred?

Dynamic Team Leaders Capitalize On The 1% Peak Performers.

_____

A lot of years ago, Heraclitus observed that, "Out of every one hundred men, ten shouldn't even be there, eighty are just targets, nine are the real fighters, and we are lucky to have them, for they make the battle. Ah, but the one, one is a warrior, and he will bring the others back."

Heraclitus provides an incredible team building formula for leaders to consider. Although the numbers might vary slightly, the concept has value.

Who are the ten percent? Who are the team members who are absorbing my time, sucking energy from the environment and making it difficult for other team members to achieve excellence. If they are allowed, the 10% sets the agenda and the standard—not what any leader desires.

Eighty percent of your people are waiting for a reason to engage themselves at a higher level. They can bring greater value but still don't understand the "why" behind what they do. As a result, they simply and routinely do "what" they do without an emotional investment.

I love the nine committed followers. Most of them are being under-utilized and are waiting for someone to recognize their potential. If only the leader would loosen the reins and let them run. They have so much energy to invest, talent to share and passion to inject; but they are unsure if they are being trusted to 'go for it'.

These '9' in '100' are vital to building a team that can perform at the highest level. Tapping their potential should be a leader's primary priority. Set the expectation, be specific about what success looks like and then get out of the way and let them perform.

Just keep a light hold on the reins so they know you are there to support them if needed.

Finally, who's your one in a hundred? Do you know who that super star is? Do they know they are super star? What opportunity have they been given to shine?

Your one in a hundred might inspire the nine to higher levels and convince the time clock punchers that it's time to take their performance to a new level. Peer pressure has incredible influence when we give it the freedom to work.

Questions to Ponder:

1. Time to do a little team assessment. Step back and figure out exactly how you might "effectimize" your team by understanding what role people fill?

2. Who is setting the standard on your team? Is it the right standard? Right person (people)?

Compassionate Accountability

Be Hard-Hearted On Mediocrity And Soft-Hearted On People

The story is told of two psychologists who worked in the same building; the taller one on the sixth floor and the shorter one on the third.

Each morning the shorter psychologist would get to the office early and wait for the tall psychologist to arrive. They would exchange cordialities and then get on the elevator, the shorter psychologist always positioning himself in front of the taller psychologist. When the elevator arrived on the third floor, the short psychologist would turn around, cut off the necktie of the tall psychologist and then rush out of the elevator.

Day after day the elevator operator observed this behavior until he could no longer resist asking the taller psychologist: "Sir, what are you going to do about that man cutting off your necktie every morning?"

The taller psychologist responded: "What should I do about it? It's not my problem!"

Seriously!? Whose problem is it??

Leaders must take responsibility for confronting all behaviors that negatively impact the culture, relationships or results.

Reward trust building behavior—listening, encouraging, taking responsibility, appreciating, producing. Commend these behaviors directly and honestly.

It's not easy. I'm challenged to discover effective ways to consistently reward these behaviors.

Confront, deal with, punish distrustful behavior like criticizing, gossiping, back-biting, loafing, rule writing, private whispering conversations, sarcasm, and innuendos (even tie cutting).

Never tolerate or overlook these behaviors. My tolerance level for these behaviors continues to decline as I get older.

I've embraced an approach that is hard-hearted on mediocrity and soft-hearted with people. You can set clear behavior expectations without beating people up emotionally. But they must understand what will and will not be tolerated.

John D. Beckett, writing in Succeeding in Business Without Selling your Soul, provides this valuable perspective: "Compassion without accountability produces sentimentalism. Accountability without compassion is harsh and heartless. Compassion teamed up with accountability is a powerful force—one which we have found can provide a great incentive to excel."

Think about your own level of emotion, listen to the tone of your voice and approach people with a humble spirit. It's not fool proof but the parent figure, boss image that creates fear will be softened a bit, making it possible for someone to listen.

Compassionate Accountability. The ability to communicate the good, the bad and the ugly—with compassion, is an art.

_____

Questions to Ponder:

1. What behaviors are rewarded?
2. What behaviors are tolerated?
3. What behaviors are universally outlawed?

(Answer those three questions and the gap will provide a pretty good indication how our environment ranks in this area.)

4. What do you need to reward more of?
5. What behaviors need to be eliminated?

Are People Better Off?

Is Your Culture Getting Better, Or Is This As Good As It Gets?

John Mackey, Co-CEO of Whole Foods, believes, "If you are lucky enough to be someone's employer then you have a moral obligation to make sure people do look forward to coming to work in the morning."

Aspiring to become a fabulous place to work reminds me of the Jimmy Carter and Ronald Reagan debate prior to the 1980 presidential election. Most political analysts agreed that the debate's winner was determined by a question Reagan asked the American people. He said:

"Next Tuesday is Election Day. Next Tuesday all of you will go to the polls and stand there in the polling place and make a decision. I think when you make that decision it might be well if you ask yourself, "Are you better off than you were four years ago? Is it easier for you to go buy things in the store than it was four years ago? Is there more or less unemployment in the country than there was four years ago?" If you answer all those questions yes, why, then I think your choice is very obvious as to who you'll vote for. If you don't agree, if you don't think that this course that we've been on for the last four years is what you would like to see us follow for the next four, then I could suggest another choice that you have."

Fascinating question, but how could it have such an impact? Because Americans believed their current condition was the result of who their leader was. People weren't enamored with their current condition so they elected a new leader.

Simple. Powerful. Thought-provoking.

Our team members normally don't get that vote. Yet, I'm sure they could answer that question without much deliberation.

How many team members choose to remain a part of your organization because they feel they are better off today than they were four years, 1 year, or 10 days ago? How many people leave because they don't feel better off today than they were 30 days or 4 years ago?

I often wonder what percent of our team would say;

"This is the greatest place you have ever seen – you would have to work here to believe it."

 Earl Weaver, the former manager of the Baltimore Orioles, gained a reputation for continually pestering and arguing with umpires. Weaver is best known for the digging question he normally asked every umpire a few innings into the game; "Is it going to get any better, or is this as good as it's going to get?"

That's a question worth asking about what it is like to work in your organization. Hopefully you can answer that question with an unequivocal, "we've only just begun." Right in line with that question is this one:

"Are your team members better off when they go home than they were when they arrived at work?"

NFL Football Coach Pete Carroll suggests, "Leadership comes down to taking care of the people in your organization and making them the best they can be, not giving up on them and never failing to be there for them."

Fully engaged, fulfilled, productive people will make us better tomorrow than we are today. Continually fine tune your culture to make this a reality.

_____

Questions to Ponder:

1. Are your team members "better off" today than they were last year? How about "better off" than yesterday? How? Why?

Like People

Balance Professional Expectations With Personal Heart

I don't mean to sound demeaning or too simplistic, but the reality is if you don't like people; believing in people, inspiring people or collaborating with people is virtually impossible. In fact, if you don't like people, another line of work might be more suitable.

People need to know you genuinely care about them and have their best interest in mind. See the good in everyone you meet. Find a reason to like your most difficult coworker. See the value your new team member brings to the team. Care about the personal lives of those you work with. Take an interest in what matters to others.

Irwin Federman reminded us that, "People love others not for who they are but for how they make us feel."

The harsh reality is that leaders who don't learn to like people will always be at a disadvantage to those who genuinely care. Those who don't care are like the Peanuts character, Charlie Brown, who said, "I love mankind. It's people I can't stand."

John Maxwell believes, "People always move toward someone who increases them and away from anyone who decreases them."

Effective leaders genuinely love people.

How simple (profound) is that?

"In my experience," says Jan Carlzon, Chairman and CEO of Scandinavian Airlines, "there are two great motivators in life. One is fear. The other is love. You can manage an organization by fear, but if you do you will ensure that people won't perform up to their real capabilities."

It's a personal thing. People want to know that a leader cares about them on a personal and professional level. Without invading personal privacy, communicating sincere concern and interest in their lives shows how much you value them as people. The leaders I've observed over the years who can achieve great things with their team know how to balance professional expectations with personal heart.

Leaders who positively impact people's lives have the guts to evaluate the effectiveness of their daily activities by the degree of love they've shared. You may love mankind, but learning to like (yes, even love) people is a cherished and impressionable quality.

Using LIKE as an acronym, here's a sure way to like more people:

Listen with your ears, heart, eyes and mind.
Show a sincere Interest in other's lives.
Be especially Kind to those you don't especially like.

Encourage people to like themselves a little better.

Lord Chesterfield, in his famous letters to his son, said something like this:

"My son, here is the way to get people to like you. Make every person like himself a little better, and I promise that he or she will like you very much."

Like people. The first step to believing in them.

_____

Questions to Ponder:

1. Were my conversations today laced with respect?
2. Did I treat others with the utmost dignity even if I wasn't treated that way?
3. Did I give people the benefit of the doubt?
4. Were my decisions based on what is right for people?
5. Did the people I interacted with feel better about themselves?

People! Rules! Principles!

Propel People Priorities Past Policy Propensity. Huh?

Henry David Thoreau put it this way, "Leaders are not obsessed with rules. Any fool can make a rule."

My freshman year of college involved a lot of 'firsts.' It was the first time I had a stranger for a roommate. It was the first time I shared shower and bathroom facilities with twenty-five (or more) other guys. It was the first time I had the freedom to attend class across the campus or choose from a laundry list of non-productive extra-curricular activities.

It was also the first for encountering foreign rules. During Freshman Initiation, the Dean of Students articulated some very clear rules to us newbies.

"The male dormitory is off limits to female students," he said, "and the female dormitory is off limits to male students. Is that clear?" (It was

1970—times have changed)

He continued, "Any student caught violating this rule will be fined $10 (this was 1970 and $10 was a lot of money) for the first time. Should you decide to violate the rule a second time, I will impose a $25.00 fine. A third violation will cost you $50 and a phone call to your parents."

That was enough to deter me from wanting to meander over to the girl's dorm for a late-night rendezvous. However, one of our more 'outgoing' classmates leaned over to me and posed this question: "I wonder how much it costs for a season pass?"

There will always be somebody who wants to play games with the rules. No matter how solid your policies are, there will always be an exception; someone to push the boundaries.

Many leaders love to produce rules to keep everyone from doing what only a few people are doing, and they plan to keep doing it regardless of the rules.

In strong cultures people will break the rules to do what's right for other people. In weak cultures, people break the rules to benefit themselves.

The ultimate question becomes; do I do what's right for the person I'm serving or protect my posterior by following the rules? Tough decision. . . unless I'm working in a high trust, empowering environment. In a fear infested environment, I'll follow the rules, so I don't get in trouble. In a safe, trusting environment I know my actions are protected and supported.

Thank author and leadership expert John Maxwell for this thought provoker: "Policies are many. Principles are few. Policies will change. Principles never do."

Let principles (values) guide your tough people decisions. They stand the test of time.

Never be bashful about using your principles to set a standard for people to attain and sustain.

_____

Questions to Ponder:

1. Is my leadership style policy driven or people driven? Think again. Be honest.
2. Where have I used policies to decide because I didn't want to make the tough people decision?
3. How can I more effectively use principles (values) to make people decisions?

"What Do You Think?"

Sincerely Soliciting Feedback Significantly Increases A Leader's Credibility.

Mark Sanborn reminds us that, "Employees who don't feel significant rarely make significant contributions."

A few years ago, Amazon was blindsided by employees going to social media complaining about the terrible workplace conditions. The CEO, Jeff Bezos, was made aware of the rumblings and responded to a New York Times article about the work conditions. Bezos wrote to his people: "The article doesn't describe the Amazon I know or the caring Amazonians I work with every day. But if you know of any stories like those reported, I want you to escalate to HR. You can also email me directly at jeff@amazon.com. Even if it's rare or isolated, our tolerance for any such lack of empathy needs to be zero."

"I want to hear from you."

"I want to know what you are thinking."

Jeff Bezos recognized a marvelous and simple way to make someone feel significant is to ask them what they think. How hard can that be?

"What Do You Think?"

When asked for advice, have you ever heard anyone say, "Oh, I don't have an opinion." Or, "Why would you ask me?"

I rarely encounter that response. Even if someone says it, inside they are standing a little taller than before you asked for their insight.

When you help someone feel significant, their confidence in you and trust in your judgement is immediately heightened. Soliciting input increases your credibility. Kind of ironic, isn't it?

I can't imagine a leader being arrogant enough to not want to seek ideas from others. Soliciting input is a marvelous path to understand what is happening and why, and creating new paths of innovation. When leaders seek ideas and truly listen, trust grows. It's that simple. Besides, why would we not be continually challenging and asking our team members how we can make things better.

I love Benjamin Zander, conductor of the Boston Philharmonic's comment, "I have no pride. I'll do anything that's necessary to get people involved. I'm a dispenser of enthusiasm." He's also the recipient of the high level of trust from his orchestra members because he values their individual contributions.

Soliciting input and ideas from people is a huge confidence builder which promotes positive interactions and trusting relationships. This simple action adds tremendous value to people's lives. A win-win to be sure.

William M. Boast, author of Master of Change, shared this perspective on the interaction between trusting relationships and new ideas: "Trust is...established when words and deeds are congruent. Trust also develops when people feel safe and secure. When thoughts and ideas are shot down and ridiculed, it doesn't take long to realize that climate is neither safe nor conducive to making yourself vulnerable. Defensive climates can be diminished by providing descriptive rather than evaluative comments, expressing feelings of caring and involvement, and being willing to actively seek out, listen to, understand, and utilize other people's perspectives."

———————

Questions to Ponder:

1. When was the last time you asked a team member what they thought instead of telling them what you thought?

2. How can you become a dispenser of enthusiasm like Benjamin Zander?

Tell It Like It Is

It's More Than Words.

"Nothing destroys trust quicker than the failure to tell the unvarnished truth," observed Tom Peters. "Despite what managers think, people can handle enormous doses of bad news."

People want to know what leaders think and believe. Don't make them guess. It's called transparency. Disclosure is powerful! Disclosure removes the mystery of what people think a leader thinks. Trust surfaces! I think it might be virtually impossible to over communicate.

A powerful reason to promote open, honest communication is that it minimizes rumors and gossip. Adopt a "no secrets" policy (confidential items excluded). Keep sensitive information confidential. Promote up-down-across communication. Listen with an open mind.

Admit your mistakes (people already know them). I figure everyone else is talking about my weaknesses and mistakes, so I might as well come clean. Admission of flaws and showing self-awareness are powerful contributors to credibility building.

Outlaw gossip and back-biting. Fumigate rumors, exaggeration and criticism.

Promote positive, encouraging interactions and behaviors. Share information openly. Be vulnerable. I believe once a relationship of trust is built, people will give you the benefit of the doubt when you make a mistake. If you are not trusted, they will not believe you even when you tell the truth.

People appreciate and trust leaders who tell it like it is— with a bit of tact and diplomacy. I remember when Pope John Paul II visited America. During a press conference, one reporter asked how the Pope could account for allocating funds to build a swimming pool at the Papal summer place. I love his quick response, "I like to swim, next question." He didn't make excuses, rationalize about the medical reasons or claim he was gifted funds from some unnamed source. No secrets - just plain old open and honest communication.

Remember the wisdom of Sam Walton;

"Communicate everything you possibly can to your team. The more they understand, the more they'll care. Once they care, there's no stopping them."

Be upfront. Tell the truth. Share your feelings. Be vulnerable. Fulfill promises.

Maintain confidences. Be open with people. Let them hear your heart.

Try it—frequently and consistently!

Jon Gordon reminds us that, "Communication builds trust. Trust generates commitment. Commitment fosters teamwork, and teamwork delivers great results."

_____

Questions to Ponder:

1. What does my team want to know - need to know?
2. What information, beliefs or insights have I not shared with my team that might be helpful for them to know?
3. Name one mistake you've made and transparently admitted to your team.

Who Messed Up?

Stupid Mistake! Let's Have Lunch.

I embrace Dave Ramsey's approach to mistakes. He said, "As a leader, if I know you care deeply, then when you screw up, I will be quick to give you a second or third chance. However, I have a very low tolerance for your mistakes when you don't care."

That's a fair leadership mentality toward failure and mistakes. Leaders need not display blanket tolerance of mistakes by dispassionate people. Mistakes made by passionate people with the right motivation deserve grace.

Failure is a constant reality in an innovative life. I'm living proof. I love asking "what if?" and then trying new, outlandish, risky, anti-establishment ideas. That, my friend, sets me up for countless failures. Hey, I've lived Mark Twain's observation that: "A man who holds a cat by the tail learns something he can learn in no other way." Some people just must learn the hard way. My life reflects Charlie Brown's experience. He said: "Sometimes I lie awake at night, and I ask, "Where have I gone wrong?" Then a voice says to me, "This is going to take more than one night."

You get the picture!

Don't advocate failure but do advocate learning. I have a favorite saying when things go wrong (failure) for a team member. Here it is–it's profound–

"Stupid Mistake. Let's Have Lunch."

People should never fear failure and a leader's job is to make every mistake a learning experience. Communicate confidence in the person and a desire to correct the error. Create a plan or process to keep it from reoccurring.

People want to work for leaders who fire them up, not who put out their fire. Placing blame puts out the fire. Finding solutions fuels the flame.

So . . . It's not "who messed up?" but "what did we learn?" Don't punish– encourage. Express loyalty and compassion for those who fail. Nourish their confidence and nurture the innovative spirit.

When I was seven I wanted to play 2nd base in baseball. Bobby Richardson, was the 2nd baseman for the New York Yankees in my childhood and I just knew I was destined to take his place someday. During an especially hot and error filled practice, my coach became irritated with my failure to field the ball and make solid throws to first base. He came running out to where I was standing, grabbed my glove and shouted, "let me show you how to do this."

Coach missed several grounders, grumbled under his breath, overthrew first base and then turned to me and declared: "you've messed second base up so bad even I can't play it." I never played second base again. Catcher became my position. The dream of attaining Bobby Richardson's fame quickly died.

How a leader handles mistakes, failures and outright stupid actions will dramatically impact people's willingness to try new things, make decisions or feel they can be trusted to act in the best interest of their team.

Consider the advice of William Dean Singleton when he advised: "Too many people, when they make a mistake, just keep stubbornly plowing ahead and end up repeating the same mistakes. I believe in the motto, "Try and try again." But, the way I read it, it says, "Try, then stop and think. Then try again."

_____

Questions to Ponder:

1. How can I better help people learn from what didn't go right?

Let's Be Clear

High Achievement Occurs In A Culture Of Clear, Stretching Expectations.

Italian Philosopher (and football coach) Vince Lombardi offered this helpful insight; "It's hard to be aggressive when you're confused." Clear expectations bring clarity to confusion.

Expectations are important to get everyone on the same page, headed in the same direction. Articulating a clear set of performance expectations eliminates people's excuses for failure or substandard performance. And, to change what people believe they can do, you must heighten the expectations.

Dr. Bell decided to put his overweight patient on an unconventional diet. "I want you to eat your regular meals for two days," he said. "Then I want you to "skip" a day. Commit yourself to this pattern for two weeks and then come back to see me. I would expect you will lose at least five pounds."

Two weeks later the man came back for his appointment. He surprised the doctor by announcing he had lost twenty pounds. After verifying the weight loss, the doctor asked, "You lost all this weight just by following my instructions?"

The man responded, "Yes, but I'll tell you what I thought I was going to drop dead on that third day."

The doctor asked, "From hunger?" "No," the man said. "From Skipping!"

Make sure your expectations are clearly communicated and understood. Never assume people know what to do and the quality that is expected. Clarity creates alignment of energies, effort and a sense of what is important.

Regardless if expectations are one sentence, sophisticated job descriptions, a poster on the wall or manuals in the break room; culture expectations are not taught through osmosis. They must be taught. They must be lived. They must be caught. People need to hear and experience them. Leaders show how they are practically applied in real life situations.

I love the challenge of moving people from where they are to a more fulfilling future by clearly establishing, communicating and reinforcing expectations and the desired path for achievement.
Hang on for an exhilarating ride!

Questions to Ponder:

1. What are your standards? What do you stand for? What won't you stand for?

2. What level of quality do you expect? What '3' things do you expect of every team member regardless of their position?

3. Think about a person who has struggled recently with their performance. Have your expectations been made crystal clear?

Coordinating the Talk and the Walk

People Look to the Leader to Be What They Expect Others to Be

John Maxwell put it a little differently. He said: "Your talk talks and your walk talks but your walk talks louder than your talk talks."

I read a story about a woman who took her young son to see Indian Leader Mahatma Gandhi. "Mahatma," she requested, "please tell my little boy to stop eating sugar."

"Come back in three days," said Gandhi.

Three days passed and the woman returned with her son.

"Young boy, stop eating sweets. They are not good for you," Gandhi said to the little boy.

Puzzled, the woman asked, "Why did you ask us to leave and come back in three days? I don't understand."

"I asked you to return with the boy in three days," replied the leader, "because three days ago, I, too, was eating sweets. I could not ask him to stop eating sweets so long as I had not stopped eating sweets."

Powerful! If I am to influence others, I must first make sure I am modeling what I want to see in others. Andy Stanley warns us that, "Inconsistency between what is said and what is done inflicts a mortal wound on a leader's influence." That mortal wound can be avoided by ensuring my convictions and actions are consistent.

People look to the leader to be what they expect others to be.

People on your team expect you to provide a healthy, upbeat, positive example of what you want the environment to be. You are the heartbeat of the culture. People want to work for leaders who fire them up, not put out their fire.

Sounds like a tough expectation. It is. One of the toughest realities of leadership is being an exemplary, enthusiastic, energetic, effervescent (optional) example. Continually. Not just when it is convenient. People are quick studies. If you only set the example to benefit you or to get what you want, the "fake sensor" goes off.

The most effective leaders never expect anything of their team they don't exemplify themselves.

Never expect higher levels of energy, creativity, commitment, positive attitude or loyalty than you are willing to deliver. When people wonder what is expected of them, they should be able to look at the leader's performance and get their answer.

My team will never be more positive than I am, more energetic than I am, more optimistic than I am—the responsibility of leadership is to set the bar.

Leaders cannot escape the example exam.

Whether you like it or not, you are under the microscope when you take on a position of authority. The leadership limelight causes people to look at you and relate to you differently. Everything you do, everything you say and everything people think you think will be scrutinized. That's why the phrase "walking the talk" has become so popular.

Consistency. Congruence. Credibility. Be who you expect others to be. Be who you say you will be. Be the message. The look on your face, the skip in your step and the sparkle (or lack of it) in your eye speaks volumes to your team. Be who you want others to be. This is a 24-7 responsibility.

The late Wendy's chairman Dave Thomas believed, "Of all the things leaders are supposed to do, none is more important than setting an example."

———————————

Questions to Ponder:

1. How can I go about 'being' the message?
2. Are my attitudes and actions consistent with my expectations of others?
3. Where can I elevate my performance to match what I expect in others?

Negating Negativity

Irreversible Negativity Causes Irreversible Damage

———————————

Bill Watterson, creator of Calvin & Hobbes, observed; "Nothing helps a bad mood like spreading it around."

Two fishermen were enjoying an afternoon at the river angling for their favorite catch. Each had a can of crabs they were using as bait. One man continually had to push his crabs back in the can while the other fisherman quietly enjoyed his experience while the crabs remained at the bottom of the can.

Mystified by the passive crabs, the frustrated fisherman asked his partner how he kept his crabs from escaping the can. "Oh, that's easy," he replied. "All you need is one crab who enjoys being at the bottom of the can and they will keep pulling the others back in."

What a fitting illustration of what negative people do to any environment. If they are free to exercise their basic character, negative people will continually pull others into the dull drums of negativity, bellyaching, moaning and groaning. And, the pity parties are frequent and expensive.

What is a leader to do?

Here's a reality: I can do all the right things, say all the right words and set the right example but there is no guarantee I can change anyone or any situation. That is sometimes a tough pill for leaders to swallow.

Here's what you can do:

Make a deal with people. "You don't be negative, and I won't fire you."

Wait. Wait. Before you run out and follow my advice read on. Here's a bit more appropriate approach.

Meet with the person privately (as soon as the negativity appears to be a repetitious behavior). Specifically explain the negativity issue to them citing behavioral examples of the undesirable attitude and conduct. Be very clear about your expectations and how the current performance is not contributing to the success of the team nor is it in line with the facility's values.

Literally, tell them to "Stop it!"

Ask for a commitment to change and mutually decide on a plan of action, follow-up and accountability. What if they disagree with your observation? Give them a little time to think about it but hold them accountable for their issues.

All of that said; let me be blunt: unless people want to shed their negativity, all the leadership strategies in the world will not work.

Here are two very pertinent questions:

Can they change?

Do they have the ability to make the required changes?

Will they change?

Do they want to? Is there any desire to get 'out of the can?'

Irreversible negativity causes irreversible damage. We owe it to the rest of the team to make tough choices. What we tolerate will be multiplied. Multiplied negativity is a catastrophe waiting to explode.

_____

Questions to Ponder:

1. Whose negativity is currently poisoning the culture?
2. Is there a desire to get out of the can?
3. How do I create a consistent behavior expectation regarding negative attitudes?
4. If I don't act, how will this person's attitude impact the team?

We Have A Crisis!

Disengaged Leader = Disengaged Team

_____

According to Gallup, only 35% of leaders in the United States are engaged. Worse yet, 14% are actively disengaged, leaving 51% 'checked out' or not engaged.

No wonder only 35% of US workers are engaged. How could we expect anything better?

Engagement - a person's commitment, involvement, passion, focused energy – is not something to be taken lightly. Gallup discovered that companies with engaged employees had 22 percent higher profitability, 10 percent higher customer ratings, 28 percent less theft and 48 percent fewer safety incidents.

Leadership engagement matters!

I love Brian Tracy's challenge to "Become the kind of leader that people would voluntarily follow; even if you had no title or position."

Face it, a team member's engagement is dramatically influenced by their supervisor's engagement – whose engagement is certainly influenced by their leader's engagement.

So, how does a leader get engaged?

First, the mission or purpose of the organization must be a compelling motivational factor in our lives. Engaged leaders sincerely believe in what they are doing and are convinced that their organization is committed to being extraordinary in what they do. The mission clearly provides the 'why' for their every action.

Secondly, engaged leaders unrelentingly want to make a difference. When work gives a leader a sense of purpose and meaning, incredible energy is infested in making people and the organization successful. When people are in a career for something less than that, the risk for disengagement is frightening. Engaged leaders are in their career to really do something not just for something to do.

Third, engaged leaders are doing what they do best every day. They are applying their strengths and capitalizing on every opportunity to learn and grow. This investment of physical and emotional energy stimulates people to a greater capacity.

One more thought.

Engaged leaders choose to be passionate about what they do. They are excited about setting the tone; the example of who they want others to be. Leaders inject people with positive energy and spirit and are excited about inspiring others to invest their minds and hearts into what they do.

The good news...this is a crisis that can be averted.

_____

Questions to Ponder:

1. Do the mission, vision and values stir my heart and inspire extraordinary performance?
2. What energizes me about my role as a leader?
3. How am I using my strengths to make a difference?
4. What am I passionate about? How am I inspiring others with that passion?

Have Fun Together

Lighten Up! Loosen Up! Laugh It Up!

David Ogilvy suggested; "Where people aren't having fun, they seldom produce good work."

Fun—A diversion from the norm. A spontaneous, energetic, enthusiastic, engaging conversation. Laughter in the hallway. A personal moment with a co-worker.

Lighthearted joking. A practical joke. A spur-of-the-moment line dance. Looking at old challenges in creative ways. A culture of relaxed enjoyment.

W. Edward Deming, the father of the Quality Evolution lamented toward the end of his life that "far too many organizations, in their pursuit of quality, overlooked the importance of joy in work." It's certainly possible to have so much fun that quality and productivity suffer. It is equally possible to create a stuffy, suffering environment where there is little fun in the pursuit of quality and productivity.

Balance. It's all about balance.

In his audio series Embracing Chaos, Tom Peters admonishes leaders to "fight bland dullness!" Create an atmosphere that is alive, vibrant and full of vitality; a happy, enjoyable place to be. Productivity experts tell us the most productive workplaces have at least 10 minutes of laughter per hour.

Here's a quantitative study you can do. How many minutes of laughter are you hearing in the hallway, office or break room? Now subtract the number of people who haven't told their faces how grumpy they are today. Just a thought. . .

Work is tough enough not to have fun. If you can't have fun in what you do, you should change what you do or find a way to interject some fun.

Bring enjoyment into the workplace. Nurturing creativity and energizing people foster trust, increases the quality of people's efforts, and improves the bottom line.

Every year, the Great Place to Work Institute asks tens of thousands of employees to rate their experience of workplace factors, including, "This is a fun place to work." On Fortune's "100 Best Companies to Work For" list, produced by the Great Place to Work Institute, people working in companies that are determined as "great" responded overwhelmingly -- an average of 81 percent -- that they are working in a "fun" environment.

Now, that's impressive! Team members working in the 'great' companies are also having a fun time doing what they are doing. At the "good" companies -- those who do not make the top 100 -- only 62 employees out of 100 say they are having fun.

That gap contains a powerful message about the impact of "fun" in a work environment.

I considered offering an extensive list of fun "how-to's." Then I realized, if someone has to tell you how to have fun, the chance of you actually trying anything is minimal.

Lighten up! Loosen up! Laugh it up!

As Dale Carnegie reminded us many years ago, "People rarely succeed unless they have fun in what they are doing."

Just trying to help you be successful.

––––––––––––

Questions to Ponder:

1. What's the 'fun quotient' in your organization?
2. How does your culture encourage a periodic "diversion from the norm?"

Overcoming An Illusion

People Are 'Down' On What They're Not 'Up' On

As leaders we really don't have a choice when it comes to communication. We either choose communication or isolation. The challenge is for our team members to 'feel' communicated with.

George Bernard Shaw suggested, "The problem with communication is the illusion that it has been accomplished."

Consider these simple leadership strategies to overcome the illusion.

1. Seek to understand

It's not what you think.
It's not what you think they think.
It's what they think that really matters.

Henry Ford suggested, "If there is any one secret to success it lies in the ability to get the other person's point of view and see things from his angle as well as your own."

Leadership begins with our ability to get inside of another person's world and to see it as they see it not how we think they see it. It would behoove us to invest more time seeing the world as others see it rather than telling them how they should see it.

2. Become a Hear-a-Holic
(I made that word up)

Leadership isn't always about having the right answers but asking the right questions. The fast track to becoming a communication expert is to learn how to ask questions. Seek continual feedback from team members. Be available. Increase your visibility. Take the time for informal interactions. Get opinions and reactions to change.

In his leadership prime, Lee Iacocca commented, "I only wish I could find an institute that teaches people how to listen. Business people need to listen at least as much as they need to talk. Too many people fail to realize that real communication goes both directions."

"Real communication goes both directions."

Are you dividing your time between verbalizing and being a 'Hear-a-Holic?"

3. Endorse Info-Mania
(I made that one up too)

Sydney J. Harris suggested, "The two words information and communication are often used interchangeably, but they signify quite different things. Information is giving out; communication is getting through."

If you don't disseminate information and tell people the facts, they will create their own. It's just human nature.

Always remember, people don't speculate on the positive side.

Responding to this principle, one leader defended his company by saying, "We are telling them. . . They just aren't listening." I can't deny that sharing information and making sure people absorb it isn't complicated. It just is but our efforts are worth refining.

Jack Stack, writing in The Great Game of Business said, "The more people understand what's really going on in their company, the more eager they are to help solve its problems."

It looks like this:

The more team members know, the more they understand; the more they understand, the more they care.
A basic principle of human nature is that people are 'down' on what they're not 'up' on.

James Humes was so right; "The art of communication is the language of leadership."

Update people on a regular basis. Keep people posted regarding the fact you have no new information. Be specific, candid and diplomatic. Squelch the grapevine by clearing up rumors and misinformation. Tell the troops how they're doing, how the company is doing. Explain 'why' things are being done.

The communication trinity is:

Tell 'em...
Show 'em...
Ask 'em...

―――――――――――

Questions to Ponder:

1. What actions can you take to ensure you know what and how people think?
2. What is your verbalizing to listening ratio?
3. What information do you have that you didn't have when you weren't a leader but wished you knew? Share that information with your team.

Build A Participative Culture

Involvement breeds commitment and commitment breeds ownership

I concur with Tom Peter's request. "I beg each of you," he said, "to develop a passionate and public hatred of bureaucracy."

Here's an example why.

Captain Edward John Smith, captain of the infamous Titanic, apparently didn't endorse the value of a participative environment. Edward John Smith had been a captain for twenty-five years when he pushed the Titanic off on its maiden transatlantic voyage.

Experts studying the disaster concluded he failed to consider the data or listen to the information and advice offered. He relied on HIS experience, HIS knowledge, HIS ego.

Captain Smith underestimated the icebergs, took too many risks and ultimately pushed the ship beyond its capabilities. He ignored all input that could have saved the ship and the passengers from their unfortunate demise.

I've learned that attempting to safely navigate the present and successfully move into the future requires me to understand the value of fully engaging people's talents, expertise, and knowledge.

Bureaucratic organizations are about the system, control, doing things by the book, not rocking the boat, and many other dysfunctional practices. These environments create barriers that severely suffocate people's passion and squelch productivity.
Ultimately, people give up, leave or even worse, stay and slowly die marching in place.

Participative cultures open the door to personal achievement and organizational excellence. Theodore Roosevelt realized that, "the best executive is the one who has sense enough to pick good men to do what he wants done, and the self-restraint enough to keep from meddling with them while they do it." These are the leaders who understand how to build a participative culture where people and organizations maximize their potential.

You'll know you have a participative environment when "we" replaces "they" and people are continually bringing new ideas to the surface for consideration. When team members take initiative to resolve problems, do whatever it takes to get the job done and find work fun and enjoyable, the signs of engaged participation are surfacing.

I love the story of the little boy who attended Sunday School every Sunday. He was well versed in the right answers to give to the teacher's questions. One morning the teacher asked, "What is brown, furry, has a long tail, and stores up nuts for winter?"

He was taken back by this unusual question. "Well," the little boy muttered, "I guess the answer is Jesus, but it sure sounds like a squirrel to me."

In top down organizations everyone is looking for the one 'right' answer – according management. In a participative environment, the process of finding new and innovative 'right' answers are paramount to the results achieved.

Engage the hearts and minds of your team and then watch them generate ideas, refine processes, innovate, and generate accomplishments previously considered unattainable. A participative environment is a powerful thing to behold and even more fun to lead.

"People tend to resist that which is forced upon them," observed Vince Pfaff. "People tend to support that which they help to create."

Questions to Ponder:

1. In what areas, can you get your team more involved navigating the organization's future direction?

2. How can you free people to discover several 'right' answers instead of the conventional 'right' answer?

Invest in the Upside

Leaders Are The Relentless Architects of People's Potential

Leaders often unintentionally reward incompetence and irresponsibility by giving these people far too much time and attention.

George Odiorne advised: "If your people are headed in the wrong direction, don't motivate them."

Who absorbs most of your time, energy and attention? The high-performance people, or those not meeting your expectations? Come on, be honest.

Are you out there developing the developable or convincing the inconvincible?

Do you have people who would be better off somewhere else? Share them with your competition. Get serious about this one. People are expected to either get happy, engaged, positive, or get off the bus!

Dave Anderson reminds us, "Some managers should wear bonnets and carry diaper bags, because in their management role, they function more as a nanny than as a leader."

It's impossible to build a world-class department or organization with marginal people who have no interest in growing—people you need to continually babysit.

That's why it is imperative to invest your time and energies into "potential" people.

Reward and recognize superstars. . .or those who can be.

Howard Hendricks advised: "Don't put live eggs under a dead chicken." I might add, "don't invest your best energies in people who have demonstrated their lack of commitment to give the best of themselves."

I've encountered far too much tolerance for underperformers. It's time to abandon that unproductive habit and expect people to perform. That's why we pay people—correct? "Free up the future" of your energy drainers. The unmotivated (or those motivated to do nothing) create an ongoing energy drain that will suck the life out of your culture.

Industrialist and philanthropist Andrew Carnegie declared,

There is no use whatever trying to help people who do not help themselves. You cannot push anyone up a ladder unless he is willing to climb himself.

Not convinced? Just remember, apathetic poor performers who are allowed to continue their employment are contagious. They will ultimately reduce the team's standards to their level. Fumigate your organization of bellyachers, moaners, and groaners. Enough said. Probably more than enough.

Move on to those enthralled with contributing to the team, expanding their talents and investing themselves in the organization.

Leaders have the privilege to be relentless architects of people's potential.

Here's the perfect combination. Reveal people's strengths and then spend the bulk of your time aligning their strengths with the needs of the organization and encouraging their development and engagement.

In Robert Altman's Oscar Acceptance Speech, he said, "The role of the Director is to create a space where the actors and actresses can become more than they've ever been before, more than they've dreamed of being."

It's the actor and actresses' job to take advantage of the opportunity. The 'heroes' will stay and the 'villains' need to go.

_____

Questions to Ponder:

1. What percent of your time is being invested creating a space, the support and tools for those who want to excel?
2. What percent of your time is being spent on people who are actively disengaged?
3. How's the balance?

Display a Humble Heart

Leaders Do the Undesirable Things Others Prefer Not To Do

Leaders could benefit from a periodic Ego Enema. That's not an attractive visual. Simple message—be the servant. Humble yourself. Don't expect your team to do anything you're not willing to do. Get rid of the ego.

Several years ago, I worked in an organization where we had all-staff rallies (in-service training) every month that required the setting up of 100 or so chairs. I normally assisted with the set-up and tear down for those meetings.

After one rally, the maintenance person who had worked in a school setting for many years and oversaw this responsibility, said to me: "You know, you are the first administrator type person who has ever helped me set up for a meeting or be willing to haul chairs."

His comment was the most valuable leadership training I've ever received and reinforced the words of Peter Drucker who suggested, "No leader is worth his salt who won't set up chairs."

James O'Toole wrote, "95% of American managers today say the right thing. 5% actually do it." Ouch!

An ego enema brings us back to what is important . . . serving those around us. At times, this means I do the undesirable things others prefer not to do.

Dr. Evan O'Neill Kane made history twice in the same day. The chief surgeon of Kane Summit Hospital in New York City was convinced that local anesthesia was a better option than the accepted practice of always using general anesthesia. Dr. Kane felt the patient sustained too many risks when completely put under.

His plan was to find a volunteer who would allow him to perform an appendectomy (an operation he had performed nearly four thousand times) with local anesthesia. The search was difficult because prospects feared the local deadening might wear off, leaving them in great pain. Others did not believe it would work.

At last, Dr. Kane found a willing volunteer. On February 15, 1921, the volunteer was prepared for surgery and given local anesthesia. The sixty-year-old surgeon performed the procedure without complications. Dr. Kane proved his point, as the patient experienced only minor discomfort. Naturally, Dr. Kane became famous as a surgeon that day, but even more interesting is the fact that he became famous for being the patient as well. He proved his theory by operating on himself!

Let me be clear, as much as I believe in the need for leaders to set the example, I have no intent of performing anything so extreme. However, I still contend that,

Leadership shines brightest when the leader does what nobody else is willing to do.

Questions to Ponder:

1. What are you willing to do that no one else wants to do?

What Makes People Thirsty?

It's not what you think. It's not what you think people think. It's what they think that really matters.

A pet food company developed a revolutionary new 'dog treat' accompanied by a sophisticated marketing plan. One year after the product hit the retail market, the sales team gathered for their annual convention.

"How do you like the product's slogan?" asked the sales manager.

"Great" ... "Innovative" ... "Eye-catching," came the replies.

"What do you think of the product?" he asked.

"Fantastic" ... "Terrific," they all responded in unison.

"What about the sales force?" he queried with a grin.

They were the sales force so, of course, they considered themselves the best in the business.

The tone of the meeting became more serious as the manager continued. "We have a dynamite product, wonderful packaging, catchy marketing and the greatest sales team in the land. So, tell me why sales rank dead-last in our industry."

The room was silent until one brave salesperson offered this insight:

"Dogs don't like the stuff."

The believing-in-people-more-than-they-believe-in-themselves stuff sounds great, but can it sell in the real world? Great question! The definitive answer is . . . it depends. It depends on whether the individual is receptive and ready to grow and expand his/her world. Andrew Carnegie believed, "You cannot rush anyone up the ladder unless he is willing to climb himself."

Author Dave Anderson believes a leader's job "is not to lead your 'horses' to water and once they get there talk them into drinking. Your job is to find out what makes your 'horses' thirsty." He has a wonderful point. The leader's job is to figure out what makes their team thirsty. If you don't know, it's time to find out.

You see, it's not what you think. It's not what you think people think. It's what they think that matters.

What's important to them?

Otherwise, no matter how creative your campaign, how good your product is or what a wonderful team of people you've assembled, if you haven't figured out what makes them thirsty, they ain't gonna drink!

Will you have people who never get thirsty for more? Probably. Will there be people who remain uninspired by your personalized approach? No doubt. Are there team members who will remain frozen right where they are, no matter how much energy you invest into them? Good possibility! What do you do?

Those who tend to never get thirsty for more will probably need to look for greener pastures. Those who thirst must be given the opportunity to 'create' greener pastures.

You have an obligation to your team and your company to maximize your return on investment by achieving outstanding results. Who can get those results? The people who want to grow and contribute. I tell you boldly to do whatever it takes to nurture these people to attain new levels of success.

Questions to Ponder:

1. Have you figured out what makes your team members thirsty?
2. Who are your top performers? What will it take to help these people move to the next level?

Huddling

Whatever You Want Most For Your Team, Be Willing To Give It.

The news headlines read: "The Miracle at Quecreek." Nine miners trapped for three days 240 feet underground in a water-filled mine shaft, "decided early on they were either going to live or die as a group."

The fifty-five-degree water was the perfect formula for death by hypothermia. One news report recounted the miner's experience: "When one would get cold, the other eight would huddle around the person and warm that person, and when another person got cold, the favor was returned."

"Everybody had strong moments," miner Harry B. Mayhugh told reporters after being released from Somerset Hospital in Somerset, Pennsylvania. "But any certain time maybe one guy got down, and then the rest pulled together. And then that guy would get back up, and maybe someone else would feel a little weaker, but it was a team effort.

That's the only way it could have been."

Miracle of miracles . . . they all came out alive - together.

This incredible story exemplifies Charles Garfield's observation that, "The difference between an average player and a great player is your willingness to sacrifice for your teammates." And of course, everyone is better when that spirit prevails.

In vibrant organizations, there is a unified spirit, a sense of camaraderie. It's all about family and a mutual interest in each other's success and well-being. Every team member's ultimate task is to see that this common bond is sustained and strengthened regardless of the circumstances.

How do leaders get there without a life or death situation forcing us to 'huddle?'

Take time to get to know people. Discover what's important to them. Seek to understand their ideas, feelings, opinions, beliefs and values. Get inside of their world. Let others know how much you value them and appreciate all they do to help the team succeed.

Let people see who you are. Be genuine. Be vulnerable. Be real. Listen to people's hearts. Share yours. Take time to connect with people. The more transparent I am the less people need to guess who I am or how I'll respond to situations. Express your heart.

Whatever you want most for your team, be willing to give it.

Be willing to give of yourself without expecting anything in return. Speak positively about your teammates, your team efforts and your achievements. Help each other win and take pride in each other's accomplishments. Go to great lengths to help others be right—not wrong.

I'm told Navy SEALs during training sometimes link arms when they do push-ups to promote going through challenges "together," rather than going it alone. The SEALs have a great saying: "Individuals play the game, but teams beat the odds."

Huddling together, supporting, trusting, sacrificing, unselfishness...all part of building a cohesive team.

_____

Questions to Ponder:

1. On a scale of 1 – 10, what is the level of unity on your team?
2. What elements of 'huddling' could use some attention?
3. What actions can you take to bring the team together?

People Leave People

People Don't Leave Positions. People Leave People.

———————

I felt an emotional tug on my heart several times during the 2009 movie release of **The Blind Side**. This semi-biographical movie beautifully portrayed the life-changing power of love.

For most of his childhood, 17-year-old Michael Ohr lived in one foster care home after another due to his mother's drug addiction. That is until Leigh Anne Tuohy happened into his life. She notices Michael walking on the road, shivering in the cold; when she learns he intends to spend the night huddled outside the school gym, she offers him a place to stay.

Michael's life was never the same. The Tuohy family accepted him, believed in Michael, encouraged him, challenged him to improve his academic performance and ultimately nurtured his athletic ability; paving the way for Michael to become an NFL star.

In many ways, The Blind Side story represents the potential impact leaders can have on people.

Every leader is unofficially charged with making a positive difference in people's lives.

Quint Studer reminds us that, "The problem is not motivation. It is the ways in which we unintentionally demotivate employees."

Any attitude, behavior or approach we take with people that undermines the exciting possibility of making a positive difference is no doubt a formula for creating "demotivation."

Here are a few:

"You should just be happy to have a job."
"I'm the leader. . . respect me."
"That's the policy —."
"Just do as you are told!"

. . . or any variation of these.

People leave people when they don't feel accepted, valued, respected, believed in or appreciated.

People leave people when their hands are tied, or ideas are suppressed.

People leave people who fail to be transparent, caring or in tune with their life.

People leave people when what the leader says is different from what they do.

A steady diet of these experiences can motivate anyone to seek a more nurturing environment elsewhere.

Questions to Ponder:

1. Who needs me to make a positive difference in their life today?

2. What actions or attitudes of mine might be spreading toxic 'demotivation' dust?

3. What one thing can I do tomorrow to accept, value, respect, believe in, or appreciate my team members?

Care Enough to Confront

Ask Before You Dictate

I applaud NFL coaching great Bill Parcel's declaration; "I think confrontation is healthy, because it clears the air very quickly."

But, as much as I agree with Bill Parcells, another football great, Terry Bradshaw probably represents the majority opinion. He flatly stated: "I don't like confrontation."

Consider this transformative attitude to approach confrontation with a different mindset.

If I care about people, it is a disservice to them not to confront issues that are keeping them from being successful or are hindering the team's effectiveness.

People want and need to know the boundaries and expectations of their role. Confrontation is not about punishing or humiliating people. It is the leader's responsibility to teach people how to meet expectations and take control of their own success.

So, what if I don't feel like confronting issues? Fine. Here is the message that will be communicated to the remainder of the team.

One, I don't care about the problem, or two, I am too dumb to notice. Just telling it like it is. . .

You might ask: What advice do you have for making my next confrontation a successful experience? Here are a few simple yet profound considerations I've found useful.

Be Factual. Ask before you dictate. Get their side. Make sure you have the specifics. . . what's real, actual and visible. Avoid hearsay or perceptions. Don't make it personal. This is not about you versus me.

Be Fair. Confrontation is not a ticket for personal attack. This is about the issues. Don't exaggerate. Stay in control of your emotions—calm and supportive. Look for solutions together.

Be Firm. Wishy-Washy is weak leadership. Tell it like you see it—with tact, compassion, and love. Be purposeful and concrete. Be responsible TO people but never take responsibility FOR their issues.

Be Friendly. Really? Friendly. Be open-minded enough to listen to the other side. Be approachable, pleasant, and non-argumentative. Be kind. Let people know you care about them.

Treat others as the most important person in your life.

Let that be the guide for every encounter you have. When you truly care about people and do the right thing, in the right way for the right reason–good things will happen.

Remember; when it's done, let it go. Move on. Don't let it impact your relationship.

_____

Questions to Ponder:

1. What behavior have I been overlooking that needs my attention?
2. Do I care enough about that person and the rest of my team to take action?
3. What am I waiting for?

Amplify Your Relational Return On Investment

Get Excited About Other People's Lives

In the movie, As Good As It Gets, Helen Hunt was tormented with ambivalence toward Jack Nicholson. On one side he is kind and generous to her and her sick son. In a flash he becomes agoraphobic, obsessive-compulsive and perpetually offensive. Helen experiences it all and in moment of desperation, she laments to her mother: "I just want a normal boyfriend."

"Oh," her mother empathetically responds, "everybody wants one of those. There's no such thing, dear."

People who enter relationships with the illusion that people need to be perfect and the relationship must be ideal, live in a world of continual disappointment and frustration. Their energies are invested in attempting to control, convert, alter and fix.

"Get it into your head," James Redfield exclaimed, "everyone who crosses our path has a message for us. Otherwise, they would have taken another path, or left earlier or later."

Approaching people who wander on to our paths as lives to be nourished and enriched frees us up from judgement and allows us to be people builders.

People builders accept rather than analyze, coach instead of criticize, and choose encouragement over evaluation.

You might ask, "How can I be a People Builder?" Here are few matchless qualities to nurture and develop.

Be Agreeable. Ever notice how many people love to argue? It's amazing how many people find it difficult to say things like, "I agree." "I love that perspective." "That's an interesting idea." "I can tell you've given that a lot of thought." And then, leave their commentary right there.

Whenever you disagree with someone, whether you mean to or not, you are challenging their intelligence and their self-esteem. The natural response for people is to become defensive, stubborn and often more adamant about their position.

Ultimately, the relationship takes a hit. So, ask yourself (even if the person is wrong), "how important is it for me to express my opinion?" It's a judgement call but being 'continually' disagreeable can suck the air out of a relationship.

Agreeing versus arguing almost always produces greater influence.

Be Accepting. Accept people for who they are; not what they could be, should be or would be if only they listened to you. This is a biggee!

Maurice Wagner believes, "At the heart of personality is the need to feel a sense of being lovable without having to qualify for that acceptance."

Accepting people naturally attracts others to you because people have an embedded need to be accepted. I've never met a person who declares, "I just want to be rejected by everyone I meet." No, no, I'm relaxed and free to be 'me' when I'm with those who accept me for who I am.

Take an interest in other people. Inquire into the events and happenings in their life. Learn their likes and dislikes. Seek out their point of view. Be understanding and considerate about their feelings. These are all wonderful expressions of acceptance and value.

Unconditional acceptance reaps unbelievable relational rewards. People's self-esteem is nourished, their confidence strengthened and their comfort with you is compounded.

Be Appreciative. When I appreciate people, they will more easily appreciate the other people in their life. Appreciation has a wonderful compounding affect.

That's probably why psychologist William James declared, "The deepest craving of human nature is the need to feel appreciated."

The common attitude is that I'll appreciate others when they appreciate me. Whoa! The Law of Reciprocity says, "When I appreciate others, others will appreciate me." Why in the world would we sit around waiting for others to appreciate us? Be the instigator!

See what's right with people and say something.

Identify and acknowledge people's strengths. Make people feel significant. Praise generously. Convey a warm attitude and friendly disposition.

Smile. Say thank you—every chance you get. Hug. Be generous with compliments. Use people's first name in your interactions. Refrain from criticizing. Write a note of encouragement. Bring out what God left in, rather than trying to put in what God left out. Get excited about other people's lives.

These are wonderful ways to show how much we appreciate people.

These interpersonal actions will have a definite RROI - Relational Return On Investment.

Ben Stein offered this valuable relationship insight:

"Personal relationships are the fertile soil from which all advancement, all success, all achievement in real life grow."

_____

Questions to Ponder:

1. How agreeable/argumentative am I?
2. What is my ability to accept people for who they are?
3. How can I improve my appreciation quotient?

Trust Me!

Trust—Leaders Go First!

_____

J.W. Driscoll indicated, "Trust has been shown to be the most significant predictor of individuals' satisfaction with their organization."

Here's the glitch: Team members don't feel trusted because organizations dream up several ways to communicate to people that they are not trusted. Thus, team members often don't trust their supervisor and the supervisor is suspicious of the team member.

It's a lose-lose situation. But, it doesn't have to be.

Let's use TRUST to illustrate five important things a leader can do to build relationships and an environment that exudes trust.

Trust First. If you want a trusting environment, begin by demonstrating trust. Will you get burned? Possibly. I certainly have but consider this:

by not trusting everyone has no effect on those who can't be trusted but has a debilitating effect on those who can be trusted. Leaders go first– Trust. What you sow, you reap.

Reward. Recognize. Reinforce. Go overboard to appreciate and acknowledge people's efforts and achievements. In the words of Arnold J. Glasgow, "A good leader takes a little more than his share of the blame; a little less than his share of the credit." Never (never) pass up an opportunity to celebrate results-producing performance.

Understand What People Need. Trust building leaders listen–often. They help people recognize and build on their strengths. People need competent leaders who know how to make tough decisions, take responsibility and get results. Show people why and how their efforts really matter. Know the person not just their position.

Show You Care. Be there for people. Express confidence in people's potential and support their hopes and dreams. Individualize your leadership based on circumstances and personal needs. Keep people 'in the know.' Display fairness, honesty and compassion. Be willing to ask: "What do you think?" And, consider the input!

Transparency. Be who you say you will be. Keep promises. Be authentic. Let people see and know your heart. Own your mistakes and admit them openly. Be accessible. Be willing to communicate the 'tough stuff.' Be a walking example of the company's values. Be Real! Make it a cordial, friendly and open environment.

When people believe they are being led by trustworthy, trust building leaders, there is a desire to use their talents to make a difference. High trust leaders generate self-responsibility, inspiration and a willingness to go the extra mile.

Just remember; trust is fragile and must be continually nurtured.

Questions to Ponder:

1. Which of the TRUST factors do I find most challenging?

2. Where could I invest some focused energy to nurture trust in my team?

It's a Culture Thing

Move Beyond Satisfaction...

Just over or under (depending on the survey) half of us are satisfied with our jobs.

Satisfied seems so generic. It's like the daily minimum requirement— keeps you going but adds nothing special.

"Best Places to Work" in America aren't staffed by 'satisfied' team members. In fact, I don't want to work in a place with just satisfied people. Do you?

Motivated, inspired, fulfilled, passionate, competent, dedicated, loyal— those are adjectives that describe the people I want to work with. Not just satisfied.

Rarely do satisfied people go beyond expectations and achieve anything extraordinary. Rarely, do they look for innovative approaches, fully engage their hearts in serving, or doggedly pursue excellence.

Fully engaged, fulfilled, passionate, productive people will make us better tomorrow than we are today. As a leader, I need to continually fine tune our culture to make this a reality.

Starbucks CEO Howard Schultz believes: "If people relate to the company they work for, if they form an emotional tie to it and buy into its dreams, they will pour their heart into making it better." Our task as leaders is to create an environment where engaged, passionate, fulfilled, productive team members want to be.

How can we tip the scales? Dr. Tom Osborne once commented that "every leader will establish a culture—either intentional or unintentional." Be intentional about creating a culture that encourages people to be the best they can be.

Consider a few culture basics.

Trust. Simply put, to earn the trust of people leaders need to treat people with the utmost respect. . . like the important people they are. Leaders must take the first step to trust people. Trusting precedes being trusted. When team members know beyond a shadow of a doubt that leadership cares about them and wants the best for them, trust naturally develops.

Foster Collaboration. Happiness, engagement and innovation will not occur in a fear infested, adversarial environment, individualistic environment. Check out this 6th Century B.C. wisdom from Aesop:

A lion used to prowl about a field in which Four Oxen used to dwell. Many a time he tried to attack them; but whenever he came near they turned their tails to one another, so that whichever way he approached them, he was met by the horns of one of them. At last, however, they fell a-quarreling among themselves, and went off to pasture alone in a separate corner of the field. The Lion attacked them one by one and soon made an end of all four.

Fostering a collaborative, collegial environment where we recognize individual value and worth dramatically impacts the livelihood and success of the team.

Freedom to Perform. Countless team members yearn for the opportunity to do what they do to the best of their ability without unnecessary intervention from their supervisor. Let it go leaders. Give people the freedom to apply their talents and abilities without your intervention. Strong leaders promote and allow personal control of the individual tasks people perform. Give it up! Let people excel at what they do and be there to support their effort.

Recognize. "I haven't had an orthodox career and I've wanted more than anything to have your respect," said Sally Field as she stood on the stage gripping the Oscar she'd just won for her role in the film Places in the Heart. The year was 1995 and I remember it well (I'm a Sally Field fan). "The first time I didn't feel it," she exclaimed, "but this time I feel it, and I can't deny the fact that you like me, right now, you like me!"

Oh, the joy of being 'liked' or even more important, being recognized for your achievements or contributions. Even the greatest stars among us need that reinforcement that what they do matters.

Honest Communication. Leaders in fabulous work environments tell the truth with heart. Seems simple enough, yet often leaders are tempted to tell people what they want to hear rather than what they need to hear. Speak the truth in love but give it to them straight.

These are basic principles. Our team members don't expect much—just the basics lived out well.

"The leader's task, then," suggested Nido Qubein, "is to create an environment that is conducive to self-motivation."

Questions to Ponder:

1. What can I do to nurture a culture where people can be productive and thus happy?

A "Random" Strategy...

Invest in your culture what you want to experience in your culture!

———————————

Bob Kerrey once suggested that, "Unexpected kindness is the most powerful, least costly, and most underrated agent of human change."

According to the Associated Press, Chuck Wall, a human relations instructor at Bakersfield College in California was getting bored with his outside assignments. A morning radio newscaster gave him the idea he was looking for when a cliché spoken by the broadcaster stuck in his mind: "Another random act of senseless violence." Wall plucked the word "violence" out of that well-known negative phrase and inserted the word "kindness."

The light bulb went off. . .Wall had an idea. He gave his Human Relations students the unusual outside assignment to go out into the community and "commit one random act of senseless kindness," and then write an essay about it. The essays were followed by creating a bumper sticker that read: "Today I will commit one random act of senseless KINDNESS... will you?" The students sold the bumper stickers for one dollar each and the profits went to a county Braille center.

For his random act of kindness one student paid his mother's utility bills.

Another student bought thirty blankets from the Salvation Army and took them to homeless people gathered under a bridge.

The idea blossomed. The bumper sticker was slapped on all 113 county patrol cars. Random act of kindness became the title of sermons, school lectures and the topic of conversation at professional associations and social gatherings.

After seeing the success of the idea, Chuck Wall commented, "I had no idea our community was in such need of something positive."

Could it be that your environment needs something positive? What if? What if leaders (and everyone else for that matter) were challenged to commit one uncommon random act of kindness next week? And the next. And the next—you get the idea.

Kindness Breeds Kindness.

Invest in your culture what you want to experience in your culture!

Questions to Ponder:

1. Let's change this up a bit...

    Action to Ponder:

    Every day, for the next 30 days, quietly commit to a random act of kindness to those who least expect it. Take the challenge. Try this random strategy on for size and watch it enrich your life and your team.

Nurturing Outstanding Performance

Invest In People Willing To Provide A Return On The Investment

Empowerment, perfectly displayed, is each team member clearly understanding the expectations of their role and taking one hundred percent responsibility to get their job done. . . and get it done right. Success comes from people who are held accountable for the results they control. No excuses.

As a leader Buck Rogers believed, "If you want people who work for you to strive for their best possible performance, give them as much responsibility as they can handle. Give them room to breathe and develop and hold them accountable for what they do."

Holding people accountable for achieving established outcomes is the epitome of effective leadership. Then comes the fun stuff...

Reward people who take on additional responsibilities and are willing to assume full accountability for their performance. These team members are the people who will put you on the map. Lean the world in their direction. Make sure they have what they need to excel.

Not everyone on your team is moving at the same pace. Treating everyone the same is anti-productive. Your go-getters get frustrated waiting for the rear-draggers to get on board or catch up.

Most teams have a make-up of people who make things happen, help things to happen, let things happen, watch things happen, stop things from happening and those who don't have the slightest clue what's happening. Reward the people who make things happen.

The greatest leader in history achieved incredible results by following this principle. Jesus had a team of twelve disciples who helped him accomplish his earthly mission but not all of them received an equal amount of attention. The Bible is clear that Peter, James and John were certainly Jesus' favorite to work with to achieve His goals. Jesus invested heavily (including a major forgiveness of Peter's denial) in this threesome and ultimately, they were powerful energizers of the Christian movement.

What team members eat up most of your time and energy—the committed and productive or the apathetic, bad attitude folks? I agree with Warren Bennis: "Don't overreact to the grumblers and trouble makers."

Stay tuned to your stars and slant the attention in their direction.

I would take that recommendation a bit further. Invest eighty percent of your time and energy nurturing, developing and rewarding the people who are passionate about contributing to the organization. Your 'leftover' energy can be used to let the non-performers know they have a decision to make.

My rationale is simple. Which group of people has the greatest potential for impacting and generating positive results? Then, why in the world would I give my best effort to the bellyachers, moaners and groaners?

Rewarding mediocre performers will cause the empowered spirit of the star performers to fizzle.

What about the uncommitted? Seriously consider "freeing up their future."

Harvey Mackay advised, "It isn't the people you fire who make your life miserable, it's the people you don't."

Peter Drucker was so right. "Any institution has to be organized so as to bring out the talent and capabilities within the organization; to encourage people to take initiative, give them a chance to show what they can do and a scope in which to grow."

_____

Questions to Ponder:
1. Who am I pouring energies into who has little chance of changing?
2. Who deserves my intense coaching and attention?
3. Who's on the bench that I should give a chance?

Tolerate or Fumigate!

That which we tolerate...is repeated and often multiplied

_____

I can't help but reflect on Dave Anderson's assertion that, "The wrong people are your greatest catastrophe, and mediocre people are your greatest drain on resource."

It has been estimated that the typical team has the following make-up:

30% Superstars – Keep Them Happy
50% Rising Stars – On the Right Path
20% Falling Stars – Energy Drainers

Regardless of the percentages, the labels might be helpful. The question is: "Where is the minimum level of acceptable performance? What is the lowest acceptable standard? And, the answer is: it must be falling stars 'IF' they are still on our team.

The second question is: Am I giving most of my time to the people who produce 80% (Superstars and Rising Stars) of the results. Or, do my falling stars (20%) suck up the bulk of my time and energy?

Smart leaders quickly establish behavioral and attitudinal boundaries. Energy is invested in what is sustaining the positive culture and people are empowered inside these boundaries to achieve desired results.

Negativity, toxic personalities and other poisons have a limited life span—like milliseconds. The best leaders establish a culture where negative attitudes and behaviors have no chance of survival. They are extinguished upon surfacing.

The leader's job is to nourish, encourage and reward superstars. Re-Recruit your winners frequently! Reinforce clear expectations and provide direction, training and coaching to your rising stars. The leader's job is NOT to lower the standards by adjusting for and accommodating the falling stars. That would be considered condoned incompetence.

I must decide on what type of person is not an asset to the team. If I don't deal with the falling stars today, my Superstars may be gone tomorrow. Even if the superstars and rising stars don't leave, they will be naturally demotivated to continue their stellar performance. What's the use! You can get more attention by not doing anything.

"The culture of any organization," suggested Steve Gruenert and Todd Whitaker, "is shaped by the worst behavior the leader is willing to tolerate."

That which we tolerate. . . is repeated and often multiplied. **Be totally intolerant of apathy, mediocrity or behaviors that conflict with the mission and values.** For goodness sake, don't reward the falling stars by giving them far too much time and attention.

The powerful, positive standards you create are also infectious. **Either create a culture that rewards your stars or falling stars will create the culture for you.**

Tolerate or Fumigate. Time to decide. **We can never build a great team around marginal people.**

As Harvey Mackay reminds us, "It isn't the people you fire who make your life miserable, it's the people you don't."

Questions to Ponder:

1. Who are my falling stars? What action do I need to take?
2. What tools, encouragement and /or resources could I provide my rising stars?
3. How can I reward and empower continued all-star performance?

Maximize People's Strengths

Help People Touch Excellence

I often reflect on Peter Drucker's sage advice: "The purpose of an organization is to maximize strengths and to make weaknesses irrelevant."

In Vince, a personal biography of Vince Lombardi, author Michael O'Brien notes that the legendary coach of the Green Bay Packers football team recognized the importance of focusing his player's attention on what they did well.

Before a game with Green Bay's archrival, the Detroit Lions, Lombardi showed films of only the successful running plays previously used against the Lions. That way, his team would be more likely to take the field with confidence.

Lombardi's teams had eight plays they ran to perfection. The opposition knew the plays but were unable to stop them due to perfect execution. The Packers were brilliant at the basics and playing to their strengths.

Lombardi experienced remarkable coaching success by establishing high expectations, ensuring players recognized and capitalized on their abilities and reaching toward flawless execution.

In his book, Now Discover Your Strengths, Marcus Buckingham delivers the powerful message to every leader that the most productive thing we can do in an organization is to help people understand where their dominant talents lie. In other words, don't try to change what people are but develop what they have. In fact, he believes, "The best strategy for building a competitive organization is to help individuals become more of who they are."

The more people touch excellence by using their strengths the less attention will be needed to correct weaknesses because they will become irrelevant.

I'm also prone to heeding Albert Einstein's observation: "Everybody is a genius but if you judge a fish by its ability to climb a tree, it will live its whole life believing that it is stupid."

How does this work?

Baseball legend Reggie Jackson once observed, "I'll tell you what makes a great manager: a good manager has a knack for making ballplayers think they are better than they are. He forces you to have a good opinion of yourself. He lets you know he believes in you. He makes you get more out of yourself. And once you learn how good you are, you never settle for playing anything less than your best."

That is a wonderful synopsis of the leader's path to maximizing people's strengths. Make every person "think they are better than they are" and you will avoid treating their genius like they should be something other than they are.

Think about this:

What if a leader invested their energies in making people's weaknesses irrelevant by making their strengths stronger?

What a revolutionary concept!

Make it happen...

———————————

Questions to Ponder:

1. Can you describe the unique talents of each of your team members?
2. What action have you taken to:
   1. Acknowledge their strengths
   2. Identify opportunities for their talents to be put to good use
   3. Recognize the contributions they make using their strengths?

People Focused Culture

Help People Become More Than They Have Ever Been Before

_____

According to countless studies, about 50 % of our team members enjoy their jobs. Happy, inspired and fulfilled team members are becoming the exception rather than the rule.

How sad!

Happiness or distaste is often a reflection of the environment and not the job itself.

To create a culture where people are inspired to invest themselves 100% because they love coming to work seems nearly impossible. Or is it?

The older I get the more convinced I am that it all begins with "treating others as they would like to be treated and as the most important person in your life."

How do you create such a culture? Here are a few Simple Big Picture Components:

Be a Place Where People Love to Come to Work.

Seriously? Seriously! Ask people: "Do you love coming to work every day?" If so, why? If not, why not? Listen.

If your organization is a lousy place to work. . . Change it—Now!

Increase the "ways." Eliminate the "why nots."

Help People Understand the Why

Mr. Starbucks, Howard Schultz suggested, "People want to be part of something larger than themselves. They want to be part of something they're really proud of, that they'll fight for, sacrifice for, trust."

If you hire people to just do a job, you'll probably get compliance. Hire people who believe in what you stand for and you'll create a movement.

A vibrant mission, inspiring vision and true to life values are pillars to create a solid people focused culture foundation. They help people understand "why" they do what they do and make them proud of the "what" and "how.".

Get the Right People on the Bus and the Right People Driving the Bus.

Here's the reality. You can help people become more of who they are but you can't make them something they're not. People don't change much.

Ensuring you have the right people with the right talent, attitude, character, passion and energy is imperative. It's called FIT.

When the right people are in their seats, everyone feels there is a collaborative desire to achieve a common mission.

Create a Fabulous 1st, 2nd, 3rd ... Impression.

What is it like for a new team member to walk in the door on their first day of work? What do the seasoned team members do to make the newbie feel at home the first day? Does the rookie go home excited to come back the second day?

People decide in a short period whether to resign from their position. They just take a while to leave.

Don't forget your "old-timers!" They still love to be impressed by how they are treated.

Establish Clear Performance Expectations and Hold People Accountable for Results.

Holding people accountable for high performance standards isn't punitive. It communicates the message that you believe in them, care enough about them and the company to never settle for less than excellence.

Unwillingness to address unacceptable behaviors communicates an apathetic attitude toward your company's performance expectations and people's ability to rise above mediocre.

Give people the freedom to do what they do best and the permission to make decisions that matter.

Believe in people. Eliminate Snoopervision. Instead empower–free up people to perform. Promote "we" rather than us vs them. When the team wins–everyone celebrates.

Provide a Place Where People Feel Valued, Important, Appreciated & Recognized for What they do.

During his Oscar acceptance speech, Robert Altman said, "The role of the Director is to create a space where the actors and actresses can become more than they've ever been before, more than they've dreamed of being."

Mr. Altman beautifully summarized the dream of every team member. It's the leader's privilege to make it come true.

Celebrate successes. Cheer people on. Build security by letting people know how valuable they are. Speak positively about your team privately and publicly. Knowledge, responsibility and praise are priceless gifts.

Ultimately, most leaders come to the same conclusion Lou Gerstner did writing in Who Says Elephants Can't Dance: ". . . Yet I came to see in my time at IBM that culture isn't just one aspect of the game–it is the game."

———————————

Questions to Ponder:
1. Do your people love to come to work? Why? Why not?
2. How do you know people know what's expected of them?
3. What specific actions do you take to ensure people feel valued and appreciated?

Removing the Obstacles

Great Leaders Figure Out What People Need, Remove Distractions And Give People The Freedom To Excel

---

Who are the great leaders in history? What made them great?

Some believe leaders are great because of the influence they have on people. Still others believe achievements made them great or because they had a massive group of followers. There are certainly several contributing factors to greatness.

One thing stands out to me.

Great leaders understand what people need and reach out to meet the highest needs.

Great leaders 'get inside' of their people and understand what they need to get jumpstarted.

Vince Lombardi believed, "Coaches who can outline plays on the blackboard are a dime a dozen. Those who succeed are those who can get inside their players and motivate."

It's true you can hire people to work for you, but you must understand and attempt to meet their needs for them to work with you. That's why giving people what they need is paramount to their personal growth and desires to accomplish more. Walter Lippmann, founder of The New Republic, said, "Ignore what a man desires and you ignore the very source of his power."

Here's an angle many leaders fail to consider. . .

Management guru Peter Drucker said, "Management's job is to find out what it's doing that keeps people from doing a good job and stop doing it." Sounds reasonable, especially considering Drucker's additional thought:

"So much of what we call management consists in making it difficult for people to work."

Remove all obstacles that negatively affect a person's ability to perform. Removing the obstacles also eliminates excuses for poor results.

I'm convinced all people are motivated. I agree with James Burke, retired CEO for Johnson & Johnson when he said: "I really believe that individuals are capable of doing a lot more than they believe they can do. Given the right environment, you can get surprising results. I believe all of us can do ten, twenty, thirty times more than we might think."

You might argue that I don't work with some of the people you do. Possibly.

I'm just too much of an idealist to believe people get up in the morning, prepare to go to work and on the way, ask themselves; "How can I mess things up today?"

People want to make a difference. Our job is to not de-motivate them by continually causing frustration. Remove the obstacles or things that frustrate people and you'll be amazed how motivated they are to perform.

So. . . how can we raise people's performance to the highest level?

Figure out what people need.
Remove the frustrations.
Discontinue de-motivating practices.

"The problem is not motivation, suggests Quint Studer. "It is the ways in which we unintentionally demotivate employees."

_____

Questions to Ponder:

1. What frustrations keep my team members from performing at their highest level?
2. What are we doing that hinders people from doing a good job?

Hold Hands

Heartfelt Leadership Is Not For The Faint Of Heart

David Gergen, writing in Eyewitness to Power, observes, "At the heart of leadership is the leader's relationship with followers. People will entrust their hopes and dreams to another person if they think the other is a reliable vessel."

Amen!

People need to know you will go to bat for them in good times and bad. They trust people who walk along side of them and help them achieve their dreams. Trust builders identify strengths and then go to great lengths to maximize people's potential by helping them use those unique abilities.

I know there are people you would probably jump off a cliff for...and those you would sometimes like to push off a cliff.

Maybe the bigger question is, "if I were standing on the edge of a cliff and a breeze causes me to lose my balance, would my team grab my arm and pull me back or gently push me over?"

Just kidding!

I'm not kidding about the necessity of a leader to sincerely care about people.

Great leaders make us feel better about ourselves when we are around them.

They are cordial, friendly, personable, and sensitive to our personal and work needs. Trust building leaders create safe environments.

I read this little story that reminds of the leader's role in supporting their team members and convincing people how much they care. A little girl and her father were crossing a bridge. The father was kind of scared, so he instructed his little daughter: "Sweetheart, please hold my hand so that you don't fall into the river."

The little girl said: "No, Dad. You hold my hand."

"What's the difference?" Asked the puzzled father.

"There's a big difference," replied the little girl.

"If I hold your hand and something happens to me, chances are that I may let your hand go. But if you hold my hand, I know for sure that no matter what happens, you will never let my hand go."

In any relationship, trust creates the bond that makes traversing through all of life's ordeals workable. A leader can grab the hand (figuratively and sometimes literally) of their team and lead them forward. Knowing someone cares enough to walk with me creates a special trusting bond.

We can't accomplish this sitting in our office at our royal throne (desk). The leader sets the tone and amount of caring throughout the workplace by making themselves visible, available and approachable. Some interactions are surface, some brief, some personal but it's face-to-face—heart-to-heart. Getting people to believe you care is hard work.

Author James Autry nailed it. "Good management is largely a matter of love or if you're uncomfortable with that word, call it caring because proper management involves caring for people, not manipulating them."

Questions to Ponder:

1. What are the names, interests, strengths of 80% of your team members?
2. Who are the other 20% and what is important in their life right now?
3. Who needs you to hold their hand through some difficult times?

Filling the Gap

Help People Know What Success Looks Like And How To Get There

Before becoming an instrument-rated pilot that allowed me to fly with autopilot, my every move as a private pilot was monitored by two critical instruments: a heading indicator and an altimeter. If I allowed the plane to veer off course, the heading indicator gave me immediate feedback and indicated the direction I needed to go to adjust and get back on course. The altimeter was equally helpful. It gave me immediate feedback on any altitude variance from my required flying altitude. Any variance of 100 feet, different from the expected flight altitude required an immediate adjustment.

There are two important factors here. First, I need to know how to get from where I am to where I want to go and what coordinates are necessary to get there.

Secondly, during the journey, continual immediate feedback keeps me on course. Arriving at my destination is often all the affirmation or recognition I needed.

Essentially, these two instruments gave me a sense of security. If I could keep the needles lined up on the expected direction and altitude, the chances were very good I would arrive at my desired destination . . . safely and timely.

What's that got to do with leadership?

Glad you asked.

Leaders help people bridge the gap between where performance is and where it needs to be? What adjustments are needed to keep us on the intended flight plan?

The practical formula for people to excel at their job, master their responsibilities and create success might look like this:

Clear Expectations + Continual Feedback + Corrective Adjustments = Commendable Success.

For years, industrial psychologists, productivity experts and workplace surveys have affirmed a few basic principles of human nature and performance. People like to know exactly what is required of them (expectations), where they currently stand (continual feedback) and what they need to do to meet expectations (corrective adjustments).

Simply stated, we like to know where we are, where we need to go and how to fill the gap between reality and expectations. Help people understand what success looks like in their position.

Leadership expert John Maxwell believes, "Leadership is the art of helping people change from who they're thought to be to who they ought to be."

The magical combination of expectations, feedback and adjustments set people up for success and get to where they ought to be.

_____

Questions to Ponder:

1. What behaviors, attitudes or measurable results are necessary for people to know they are 'on course?'
2. Ask three people you lead: "Do you have a clear picture of the performance expectations of your position?"
3. What adjustments might be needed to help people achieve the desired destination?
4. When is the last time you provided feedback (positive or corrective) on someone's current direction? Who could benefit from a corrective adjustment?

Blah...Blah...Blah...

What Do People Need To Know? What Do People Want To Know? Tell Them. . .

Decades ago, Peter Drucker observed; "Sixty percent of all management problems are the result of poor or faulty communication."

Ouch! It takes special talent to consistently deliver a powerful, penetrating, personal message.

In the pioneer days Native Americans were masters at communicating with smoke signals . . . or at least that is what I've been told. Two young braves living in the same village were sending smoke signals to their girlfriends in a distant village. The first brave carefully prepared his romantic message and began sending it. Just as he finished, a dynamite blast occurred in a nearby mine creating a giant cloud of smoke.

The girlfriend of the second brave looked at it and said to her friend, "I wish my boyfriend could communicate like that."

The value of communication is in the perception of the receiver. As Andrew Grove, chairman of Intel Corporation, puts it, "How well we communicate is not determined by how well we say things but by how well we are understood."

If I can deliver effective, clear, timely, understandable messages, there is a good chance I can fill the proverbial communication "gap." If it isn't understood, it certainly won't be considered important, remembered or implemented.

Communicate your messages in a way that the team understands what is being said and allows them to support (or question) the message. Allow (even encourage) people to ask questions, disagree, argue or offer suggestions.

Interaction breeds understanding; that leads to action.

Effective communication means there is a mutual understanding (not necessarily agreement) of the message being sent. Then, we can work on support for the message and ultimately take action. But first, understanding is critical.

People normally cannot have too much information. Every team member has the need to know as much as possible. The more everyone understands what leaders, the company and their department is up to (and why) the more commitment we will experience. Continually look for opportunities to clear up rumors, squelch the grapevine, and eliminate gossip, by satisfying people's craving for information.

Experiment with ways to do it better so people have a clear understanding of the message.

Otherwise, it's just Blah! Blah! Blah!

_____

Questions to Ponder:

1. What do people need to know to better understand "why" they do what they do and/or "why" you do things the way you do?

2. What would people like to know that I've failed to tell them?

3. What would be nice to know that it seems only leadership know?

The Great Morale Debate

Be A Morale Stimulation (Not Suppression) Leader?

I must admit, sometimes I want to agree with American sociologist Larry Kersten when he suggested: "Sometimes the best solution to morale problems is just to fire all the unhappy people." Then I come to my senses and realize the challenge of managing morale is a bit more sophisticated than that.

Morale reflects a person's attitude or mental confidence with the organization. Gallup expands on that definition believing morale is "the emotional attachment or sense of engagement someone has for their job."

Simply stated, do people like working where they work, and would they recommend other people come to work where they work? If not, why not?

President Dwight D. Eisenhower was probably right; "The best morale exists when you never hear the word mentioned. When you hear a lot of talk about it, it's usually lousy."

Consider three profound imperatives for creating a high morale environment.

First, people need a sense of purpose.

"Why" do I do what I do? What is the end result? What difference am I making in people's lives? Does my contribution have any significant impact on the overall success?

People need more than a 'job.' A title, job description, and paycheck are not enough to generate high morale. Morale is directly tied to a person's opportunity to be productive and contribute to something bigger than themself.

Secondly, help people become an expert in one area of their job.

Encourage them to know more about something than anyone else on their team. Mentor them to become the specialist, the go-to person, the in-house whiz. Morale certainly isn't an issue when I'm considered the master at what I do.

Finally, give people the freedom to do their job.

Controlaholic supervisors suck the living energy out of people. Let people do what you've hired them as a professional to do. Period. No excuses. Let go of your tight controls and work with whatever the outcomes are—make it a teaching moment.

Think about it—are you a morale suppression or expansion leader?

As Harry Beckwith observed; "Morale has the qualities of an airborne virus—it leapfrogs walls and cubicles and moves through the ductwork." How true.

Invest your energies in helping people identify a sense of purpose, feel your support to become a specialist and then be given the freedom to do what I know best how to do. Then, let the virus do its thing.

———————

Questions to Ponder:

1. Does my team understand the purpose of their roles?
2. How can I help people pursue their potential?
3. What steps can I take to get out of the way and let them do their job?

Mysterious Principle

Leadership Is More Relational Than Positional

A colleague gently confided in me years ago that some people felt I was not easily approachable. I was devastated! I had always prided myself in being able to talk to anyone, respecting the worth and value of every person I encountered and open to the ideas, opinions and thoughts of other people. What could he mean by 'people were uncomfortable approaching me?'

"You move too fast and give the impression you don't have time for people," my colleague expounded.

I worked tirelessly to improve my approachability and reinforce the impression that I was available for anyone anytime.

There were still people who seemed threatened by me and nervous in my presence.

Exasperated, I approached my supervisor. "I'm really struggling," I began. "I've worked my tail off to prove I am a like-able, approachable, normal kind of guy. Yet, there are people who seem afraid of me."

My ex-high school principal supervisor replied with this piece of advice: "No matter how outgoing, friendly and gregarious you are, there will always be people who are afraid of you simply because of your position and/or your title."

Could it really be? Absolutely! I've come to call it the Mysterious Principle of Positional Influence.

Leonard Bickman conducted a fascinating experiment testing the relationship of obedience and authority. Bickman established a scenario where he had a person stop pedestrians in the street and say, "Hey, you see that guy over there at the parking meter. He's over parked but doesn't have any change. Give him a dime." Then the planted person would turn and walk away.

Bickman repeated the experience, only this time the person telling people to give the person a dime was dressed in a security guard's uniform.

The results were dramatically different: 42 percent of the people complied with the plain-clothed man, while a whopping 92 percent complied when the request came from the same man dressed in a security guard uniform.

Position can produce a personal evasiveness or caution. It also has the capacity to influence people toward action. Authority, position, title, matter. That's a good thing...and a bad thing.

A Gallup organization study, based on interviews over 25 years with 12 million workers, found that an employee's relationship with a leader significantly influenced an employee's length of stay with an organization.

A Saratoga Institute study discovered that a leader's behavior was the number one factor determining an employee's happiness at work.

As the old saying goes, "people leave people, not positions."

The leader who can build trusting relationships and communicate a belief in peoples' abilities can circumvent the adverse side of title or position.

David Gergen, writing in Eyewitness to Power, suggests that, "At the heart of leadership is the leader's relationship with followers. People will entrust their hopes and dreams to another person only if they think the other is a reliable vessel."

So, there it is. Leaders can achieve a level of compliance and thus produce results just due to their position.

Effective leaders capitalize on their position to build relationships that inspire people to unprecedented levels of performance.

It's not simple but the ability to combine authority with relational expertise produces wonderful results.

———————

Questions to Ponder:

1. How have you relied on your position to get things done without thinking about the impact on the relationship?
2. What actions can you take to bring these forces together?
3. What are you doing to build trusting, solid relationships with those you supervise?

Hobgoblin of Fools

Leadership Is Not A One Size Fits All Mentality... It's A One Size Fits One

My children are wonderful (of course they are) – and very different. As they were growing up, I didn't treat them the 'same.' I dare to bet that is true for most parents. Any attempt to treat them equal would have been disastrous. Their mother and I were particularly careful to treat them each according to their uniqueness, not their sameness. I'd advocate the same approach with team members.

Every person I work with is special. And, I plan to treat them that way. But not the same. "Oh, my goodness," you say, "how inconsistent." Emerson said: "Consistency is the hobgoblin of fools." Consistency is not the goal. Treating people as special individuals is.

I tend to believe that consistent inconsistency is the most consistent form of consistency.

You might need to read that again. . .

Take it from someone smarter than me—Vince Lombardi. This great football coach believed, "There is nothing so unequal as the equal treatment of unequals."

(You're just going to have to stay with me on this topic. It might take a couple of readings for you to understand as it has taken me decades to achieve clarity on this topic)

I know. I know. I know. This way of life has challenges. It's tricky— personally, legally, and professionally. It can get messy! A sincere desire to do 'what's right' for people inevitably surfaces the question of equity— there's that word again—and even justice. Consider the impact to the entire group and the individual. Then, consistently do what's right for people—as a group and individual.

In my world, everyone will continue to get special treatment, but no one gets equal treatment.

I'll deal with the obvious perils and tricky decisions. I fully understand the multitude of variables that need to be considered for every decision. And yes, I'm aware of the heat that sometimes accompanies treating people as individuals and not a herd to be managed.

Not everyone on your team is moving at the same pace. Treating everyone the same is anti-productive. Your go-getters get frustrated waiting for the rear-draggers to get on board or catch up. Most teams have a make-up of people who make things happen, help things to happen, let things happen, watch things happen, stop things from happening, and those who don't have the slightest clue what's happening. Reward the people who make things happen.

If you are building personal relationships with those you work with, they will come to realize you will do what's right for their teammates and for them when their time comes. I'm not sure Oliver Wendell Holmes was talking about this issue when he said, "The young man knows the rules, but the old man knows the exceptions," but it's perfect for clarifying the special treatment issue.

As leaders, we have the privilege of equipping people with what they need to become autonomous, empowered, and effective. Leaders are in the business of building high performance people. A more flexible, people-focused environment will help liberate people to do whatever it takes to make your team successful.

My attitude working with my team is this...everyone gets treated as a special individual.

Leadership is not a one size fits all mentality—it's one size fits one.

Individualize. Individualize. Individualize.

_____

Questions to Ponder:

1. How can I personalize my leadership approach so I'm meeting the needs of individuals?

2. What specific actions can I take to ensure that "one size fits one?"

Do It For The 97%

People Are Starving For Your Applause

Walmart founder Sam Walton's advice decades ago remains relevant today. "There's no better way to keep someone doing things the right way," he said, "than by letting him or her know how much you appreciate their performance."

A naïve supervisor once asked me, "Why should I tell people they are doing a good job when they are just doing what I pay them to do?" That question can be answered with another question. Do I want the performance to continue or be repeated? Behavioral science teaches us that performance that gets:

Reinforced...
Recognized...
Rewarded...gets
Repeated.

How about this anti-recognition argument: "Recognition will just go to their head."

Reinforcement will go to the heads of 3% of your people. For the other 97%, Positive Reinforcement provides a higher standard people will strive to live up to.

"I'm very good at recognizing my entire team."

Are you hoping everyone gets it? Group recognition rarely hits the target.

Personalize. Personalize. Personalize.

A group of supervisors were asked to respond to this statement: "I let my team members know when they are doing a good job." Their team members were asked to respond to a similar statement: "My supervisor lets me know when I'm doing a good job." A scale of 1 to 5 was used where 1–never and 5–always.

The supervisors rated themselves a 4.3. The team members rated their supervisors 2.3!

Surprise! Surprise!

I'm not concerned with who is right or wrong in this survey. That's not the issue.

The perception of the team is what counts.

Here's a reality check: For every positive recognition a supervisor gives, they receive only half of the credit for giving it. When I fail to give recognition, I sense the impact is multiplied.

I read a newspaper story about an old carnival headliner nicknamed "Cannonball." In his younger days, he was blasted out of a cannon 1200 times, pulled a 90-pound weight across a table with his eyelids, and performed many other bizarre stunts. When asked why he did such things, he replied, "Do you know what it is like to feel the applause of 60,000 people? That's why I did it over and over."

There might be someone on your team who is starving for applause from just one person. Could that be you?

Remember: Where there are no consequences for poor performance, the wrong actions will continue.

Where there is no reinforcement for desirable performance, the right behavior will cease.

_____

Questions to Ponder:

1. Some leaders are so preoccupied with making sure their team members are not doing the wrong thing that they overlook the right things they are doing. What winning performance did I fail to individually recognize this week? Are there star-studded performances I've come to expect? Are they being overlooked?
2. What behavior would I love to see repeated?
3. Commit yourself to providing personalized recognition to at least one person every day for the next '30' days.

You Are The Hope

People Love Leaders Who Sincerely Want The Best For Them

Louie DePalma would never earn the Boss of the Year Award. Louie was the greasy, disliked, irritating overseer of the cabbies on the television series Taxi.

Most of his cabbies had ambitions beyond the Sunshine Cab Company. But Louie saw them all as eternal cabbies. He constantly berated their dreams, squashed their aspirations and harassed them to the point of making their job life miserable.

In the episode "Bobby's Big Break," aspiring actor Bobby Wheeler is offered the opportunity to be in a soap opera. He quits his taxi day job, tears up his cab driver's license and escapes to pursue his dream. Of course, Louie is enraged (how could anyone leave his magnetic leadership style) and expresses his lack of support by boldly announcing, "He'll be back... they all come back! The only one who never came back was James Caan...and I'm still waitin!"

Unfortunately, Bobby loses the acting gig and does what he doesn't want to do—asks for his cabbie job back. Louie gloats and runs around chanting, "Bobby's a loser...a loser...a loser."

Louie certainly didn't embrace Bernard Haldane's belief that, "To get the best out of a man you must look for the best in him." I find this advice a great way to jumpstart the future for people. Look for the best in them...

Leaders who believe in people invest in people. They support their hopes and dreams and aspirations. They understand that getting more out of people depends first and foremost on believing in them and investing in their lives and futures.

Fully engaged people believe they can build a better future than the past and they believe they can directly impact that brighter future. A priority for me as a leader is to reinforce those hopes and beliefs and help to instill the confidence in people to achieve them.

Research is conclusive that people focused leadership is powerful. Yet, why is it that so many "Louies" are still in leadership roles? People are not expendable commodities. They are a rich resource of talent, abilities, ideas and potential. Any leader who doesn't get that doesn't deserve their position.

I'm recharged as I remember First Lady Barbara Bush reminding us, "If human beings are perceived as potentials rather than problems, as possessing strengths instead of weaknesses, as unlimited rather than dull and unresponsive, then they thrive and grow to their capabilities."

Most people want to love what they do where they do it. They want to invest their hearts and minds into what they do every day.

But people are hesitant to love something or give wholeheartedly to something that doesn't support them back.

Show people you have their best interests at heart. Sincerely care about the present and support their future. Inject people with your energy, passion and believing spirit. People love leaders who believe in their ability and inspire them to fulfill their potential.

You are the hope someone needs!

_____

Questions to Ponder:

1. Do you know the hopes and dreams of three people you lead?

2. What one dream can you help and encourage someone to accomplish in the next twelve months?

"Grab Butts"

Be transparent. Be genuine. Be vulnerable. Be real.

"If you're going to play together as a team," declared Vince Lombardi, "you've got to care for one another. You've got to love each other. The difference between mediocrity and greatness is the feeling these guys have for one another."

I read about a college that offers a course called Environmental Science, a sophisticated title for a class about the outdoors. The class syllabus includes several field trips including a long hike in the mountains navigating several steep trails.

One year, to prepare the students for the hike, the professor used a rather unconventional training exercise.

He gathered all the students in a wide-open area and announced these instructions: "I want you to mingle around and grab each other's butts."

You can imagine the reaction. Hesitancy. Nervousness. Curiosity. Embarrassed chuckles. But, they made the best of the situation and followed the professor's request.

Once the students had a 'feel' (pardon the poor pun) for the experience, the professor shared his rationale for this unusual exercise.

"We are going to be walking up a steep, narrow, slippery slope," he explained. "Because of this, we will have to hike single file, hunched over, using our hands and feet. If the person in front of you should slip, the first thing you will encounter is his or her butt. If that happens, you will need to reach up with both hands, grab on to both cheeks, and stop him or her from falling. If you're uneasy touching someone's butt, you might be tempted to step aside and let the person slide. This would put him or her in immediate risk of severe injury, as well as those behind you."

I recognize a marvelous team building principle embedded in this story. While I certainly wouldn't condone 'butt grabbing,' every team member can benefit from getting closer to their co-workers, so they are better able to respond in time of need. Team members who keep their distance and avoid really getting to know their co-workers are by-passing a critical and rewarding team building opportunity.

Professor Howard Hendricks said,

"You can impress people from a distance, but you can only impact them close up."

Let people see who you are. Be transparent. Be genuine. Be vulnerable. Be real.

Listen to people's hearts. Share yours. Take time to connect with people. The more transparent I am, the less people need to guess who I really am or how I'll respond to situations.

You are setting the example for the team to follow.

_____

Questions to Ponder:

1. How close is your team to one another?
2. What actions can you take to help the team get to know each other a little better?
3. How can you become more comfortable with each other?

"Don't Make Me Guess"

Share Your Heart...With Clarity

"If you have an important point to make," declared Winston Churchill, "don't try to be subtle or clever. Use a pile driver. Hit the point once. Then come back and hit it again. Then hit it a third time–a tremendous whack."

Carmen Berra, Yogi's wife of 65 years, asked him one evening; "Yogi, where would you like to be buried?"

The couple were aging and Carmen felt they needed to be making such decisions.

Yogi put his hand to his chin, thought for several minutes and told Carmen it was too tough to immediately answer. He needed to sleep on it.

The next morning, Yogi woke up, and Carmen asked him if he reached a decision.

"Yeah, when I die," Yogi said, "just bury me where you want."

"Surprise me."

(As told by MLB Columnist Bob Nightengale - USA Today 9/24/15)

That was Yogi! Just another Yogi-ism. Comical. Nonsensical. Heart-warming. Always entertaining. There are more.

"It ain't over 'til it's over."

"Ninety percent of this game is half mental."

Yogi became a cultural icon, quoted philosopher and beloved friend by saying things like this that he said, "just came out."

That's how Yogi shared his heart.

Leaders need to be a bit more specific when sharing their heart.

I was in a team meeting one day discussing an issue that had the potential for becoming volatile and divisive. I found myself vacillating on both sides of the issue. A courageous (and frustrated) team member finally said with a desperate need for clarity, "Glenn, just tell me what you want me to do. Don't make me guess."

During World War II Great Britain was being repeatedly bombed. Britain citizens feared they would ultimately have to wave the white flag in surrender. They desperately needed to hear a clear message from their leader.

One day Prime Minister Winston Churchill decided it was time to address the nation. He made a powerful (and what is now famous) speech. "We shall defend our Island, whatever the cost may be," he said. "We shall fight on the beaches, we shall fight on the landing grounds, we shall fight in the fields and in the streets, we shall fight in the hills; we shall never surrender."

Like the message or not, Churchill was clear, confident and succinct. No one had to guess what Churchill's convictions were.

Yogi Berra also said, "In theory there is no difference between theory and practice. In practice, there is."

Thank you Yogi! How true that is when discussing effective communication.

Leaders need to share their heart with clarity! People want it. People expect it. People need it. Even if they don't like the message they hear.

_____

Questions to Ponder:

1. How clear have you communicated your 'heart' message?
2. Does your communication reflect the clarity of a Yogism or a Churchill declaration?
3. Who on your team is brave enough to give you feedback on your communication effectiveness? Don't be afraid to ask for feedback.

Be You!

Influential Leaders Are The Real Deal

———————————

Admired NCAA Basketball Legend John Wooden advised, "Be yourself–no posing or pretense; be comfortable in your own skin; avoid judging yourself in comparison to others; and hold fast to your principles and ideas."

Let me Illustrate.

Ugly Betty. Not exactly a label I would envy.

The awkward but savvy and hardworking Betty Suarez from the comedy Ugly Betty embraced the label and the role, setting out to succeed in the cutthroat world of high fashion.

Betty is oblivious to fashion or style, frequently garbed in mismatched outfits, excessively bold colors and unbecoming ensembles that made her the perfect hire. The owner of the fashion magazine MODE hired Betty to become his womanizing son's (Daniel) personal assistant knowing he could never be attracted to this unattractive candidate.

Betty was purely Betty—motivated, positive, fresh and filled with an unwavering passion to bring life to the cold corporate world. Although slightly clumsy (it had to be those crazy glasses) she remains well-grounded on trying to improve herself while bringing value and a breath of fresh air to her job. She also prevents temptation from distracting the editor-in-chief, the original single purpose for her being hired.

Ironically, Betty becomes far more influential at MODE than when we're first introduced to her initial character. She never became a fashion queen, beautiful model, or intent on fitting in. Betty worked her tail off continually getting better at every task that was thrown her way. Most importantly, Betty remained true to her core—her authentic self.

Julius Charles Hare once advised:

"Be what you are. This is the first step toward becoming better than you are."

Leaders are visible. Their character is continually on display. Like it or not, every action, decision and communication is being weighed. Influential leaders are the real deal.

Imperfections. Insecurities. Inadequacies.

No pretense. No pretending. No promising without delivering.

Ironically, Daniel ultimately saw the real beauty in Ugly Betty. She became his confidant, internal compass, friend and at the end of the series, it appears some romance could be on the horizon.

Author Brad Lomenick reminds us, "people would rather follow a leader who is always real versus a leader who is always right."

Followers don't require perfection from their leader. They prefer and respect a leader who is willing to show their emotions, accept their limitations and be vulnerable enough to let people see their authentic self.

Finally, psychotherapist Jane Shure adds this insight, "If we buy into the notion that we are supposed to be like someone else, different from how we are, we are headed for trouble. We are not the same, nor should we be."

Be You!

_____

Questions to Ponder:

1. What can you learn from the example of Ugly Betty?

Refrain From "Snoopervision"

Eradicate Snoopervision Before It Suffocates People

Miles Anthony Smith aptly observed, "Micromanagement is the destroyer of momentum."

Micro managers (I call them Snoopervisors) possess the incredible ability to deflate any high energy, productive team member and render them immobile. (May I never fall victim to becoming a snoopervisor).

Frances Hesselbein rightly declared, "dispirited, unmotivated, unappreciated workers cannot compete in a highly competitive world."

Snoopervisors can unconsciously create all Hesselbein's undesirable indicators with a single micromanaging swoop.

Trust-building leaders have the sense to surround themselves with outstanding people and the self-restraint not to meddle with how they do their jobs. Micromanagers have their fingers in everything and subtly (or not so subtly) communicate a non-trusting attitude. They are snoopervisors---continually snooping, hovering and waiting for a mistake to be made. Snoopervisors have a relatively small parameter of "the right way" of doing things...their way.

It just doesn't make sense to me to hire incredibly talented and smart people and then invest my energies telling them what they need to do and how they need to do it. I would assert that micromanagement indicates you've hired a team of losers, incapable of making decisions, achieving goals or mastering their jobs without supervisor intervention. Back off quickly--Good people will exit this suffocating style of leadership.

Besides, what does that tell you about your hiring ability?

Remember Russ Perot--chairman of Electronic Data Systems? Here's his take on leadership's responsibility:

"First you have to have an environment of mutual trust and respect. You need to have an environment that taps everyone's creative potential. It's terribly important that you not turn bright, able people into robots by giving them procedure books and checklists."

This advice is difficult for micromanagers to swallow but it is imperative they find a way to digest it. If you want to lose high performers, become a control-a-holic.

Continually look over people's shoulder and nudge or push them along. If you want your best people engaged, learn to let go. Establish the expectations and give people the freedom to do what they do best.

I may think I have control. In reality, I have less control than those I supervise.

They determine the quality and quantity of their work. Each person decides what to do and what they would rather not do. People individually decide how motivated or engaged they will be. All I can do is encourage, inspire, influence, mentor and correct to get people to do what I need them to do.

Desired results are driven by high trust, low snoopervision, not the reverse. Author and CEO Max DePree believes, "we must trust one another to be accountable for our own assignments, when that kind of trust is present, it is a beautifully liberating thing!"

Amen!

Questions to Ponder:

1. Am I looking over anyone's shoulder? Explain to yourself why you are doing that. . .
2. What will it take for me to give people the freedom to do what they do—without my snoopervision?
3. Think about it. What can you do to let go and let people shine?

Inspiring Greatness

Are You Asking People To Do Something Great?

Tom Peters suggests, "Leadership means vision, cheerleading, enthusiasm, love, trust, verve, passion, obsession, consistency, creating heroes, coaching, and numerous other things."

I would submit that, one of the numerous 'other things' is asking people to do something great.

The movie Lincoln reinforced what an effective leader, communicator and influencer President Lincoln was. The story is told that during the Civil War, Lincoln frequented a church not far from the White House on Wednesday nights. He was given permission by Dr. Gurley, the pastor to sit in his study with the door open to the pulpit so he could privately listen to the sermon.

After one service, Lincoln and a companion were walking back to the

White House. The President's companion asked, "What did you think of tonight's sermon?"

"Well," Lincoln responded, "it was brilliantly conceived, biblical, relevant and well presented."

"So, it was a great sermon?"

"No," Lincoln replied. "It failed. It failed because Dr. Gurley did not ask us to do something great."

A primary responsibility of a leader is to never accept the world as it is but what it could be and invite people to join the journey to do 'Something Great.'

Steven Jobs, cofounder of Apple, believed: "Management is about persuading people to do things they do not want to do, while leadership is about inspiring people to do things they never thought they could."

I love that comparison! It is a fabulous philosophical and purposeful benchmark for aspiring leaders.

Leaders provide the spark that ignites people's interest and passion to become more than what they are...or even what they ever thought they could be. It is hard work!

Leaders, you are the key to inspiring greatness in others. Henry Kissinger was right:

"The task of the leader is to get his people from where they are to where they have not been."

What a privilege!

Questions to Ponder:

1. When is the last time you encouraged someone to do "something great?" Who's next?

2. In what areas can you inspire people to become and do more than they ever thought they could?

A little about the old guy...

Glenn Van Ekeren is the President of Vetter Health Services in Omaha, Nebraska, a company committed to providing "dignity in life" for the elderly. He is a frequent speaker on leadership and principles for maximizing people and organizational potential.

He is the author of a number of books including **12 Simple Secrets to Happiness**, **Speaker's Sourcebook I and II**, **Love is a Verb** and is a featured author in several **Chicken Soup** books.

For more of Glenn's wit, humor, and inspiration, follow Glenn's blog on enthusedaboutlife.com.

Made in the USA
Middletown, DE
29 July 2020